CHARLEMAGNE AND BAPTISM:

A STUDY OF RESPONSES TO THE CIRCULAR LETTER OF 811/812

GLENN C.J. BYER

CHARLEMAGNE AND BAPTISM:

A STUDY OF RESPONSES TO THE CIRCULAR LETTER OF 811/812

For Laurier, Margot & family

To fellow-workers in the vineyard

With gratitude for friendship and support through the years

GLENN C.J. BYER

International Scholars Publications
San Francisco - London - Bethesda
1999

Library of Congress Cataloging-in-Publication Data

Byer, Glenn C. J.
    Charlemagne and baptism: a study of responses to the circular letter of 811/812/ Glenn C. J. Byer.
      p. cm.
    Includes bibliographical references and index.
    ISBN 1-57309-370-X (hardcover ; alk.paper) ISBN 1-57309-369-6 (pbk.)
  1. Baptism—History—Middle Ages, 600-1500. 2. Charlemagne, Emperor, 742-814—Correspondence. 3. Church and state—Holy Roman Empire—History—Middle Ages, 600-1500. I. Title.
BV811.2.B94   1999
265'.1'09021—dc21

99-10372
CIP

Editorial Inquiries:
International Scholars Publications
7831 Woodmont Avenue, #345
Bethesda, MD 20814
website: www.interscholars.com
To order: (800) 55-PUBLISH

This work is dedicated to my Dad:
having undergone his own passion,
he now knows the real meaning of baptism
and so lives the kingdom of God.

TABLE OF CONTENTS

TABLE OF CONTENTS - CONTINUED

LIST OF ABBREVIATIONS

ALW	Archiv für Liturgiewissenschaft
CCL	Corpus Christianorum, Series Latina
DHGE	Dictionnaire d'histoire et géographie ecclésiastiques
EL	Ephemerides Liturgicae
MGH	Monumenta Germaniae historica
PL	Migne, Patrologiae cursus completus, Series latina
RB	Revue bénédictine
StT	Studi e testi

LIST OF TABLES

Commendatory Preface

The Carolingian era remains a vital one for liturgical study, stimulating as it did vast numbers of documents still waiting to be examined. Dr. Byer has provided liturgical scholars a solid, thoroughly-researched work which makes a strong contribution to this field, particularly Carolingian baptismal rites.

Originally his doctoral dissertation at the Pontifical Liturgical Institute at Sant'Anselmo in Rome, Cha rlemagne and Baptism: A Study of the Circular Letter of 811/812 demonstrates a meticulous concern for detail and a welcome clarity of presentation and analysis.

Three significant achievements mark Dr. Byer's fine study:
1) his use of the synchronic method of liturgical analysis (studying works from the same period in history to reveal the broader strokes of liturgical practice and variety in a particular historical moment);
2) a practical, political grasp of the reasons for Charlemagne's Romanization of the liturgy; and
3) a presentation of the marvelous and surprising diversity of the baptismal rituals of the era.

I commend this work to serious students of liturgy as a unique and richly-informative view of the development of the initiation rites in the Carolingian period.

Sharon McMillan, SND
St. Patrick Seminary
Menlo Park, CA

PREFACE

To take up the study of the Carolingian era is to enter an almost mythical world dominated by one man. The person of the emperor has been surrounded with legend and even his name is rendered in most languages with his greatness, Charlemagne in French and English, Carlomagno in Italian and so on. His influence is seen as the basis for wholesale changes in the life of his society and his faith. His blunders are also presented to us as larger than life, affecting the lives of thousands.

The first part of this book tries to place us in that world. The first chapter establishes who were the important people and what were the documents that will enter into this study. The second chapter tries to examine a little of who this Holy Roman Emperor was, and how his empire and the church within its borders functioned.

This book then opens up the documents concerning one moment of his life, towards the end, when he took up the question of the preparation and celebration of baptism in his realm. This may seem to be rather an insignificant item, but it proves to be revelatory on many levels. By looking at the letter he writes on baptism, and at the responses he receives to his letter, we see how he deals with the issues surrounding baptism, we get a glimpse into what kind of empire he ran, what kind of church he longed to have and how he saw his role was in salvation history.

The second part of this book tries to analyze these works, looking at the whole known span of documents on baptism form the era and sifting out the letter of Charlemagne and its responses. These chapters lay out a whole range of documents that describe baptismal rituals of a surprising variety.

The third part of the book takes up the task of seeing what these different rites have in common and what holds them apart.

There can be no doubt that the emperor saw himself as having an important role in that history, but the conclusions of this work will show that there is a need to nuance what we have thought about the way he saw himself in the world. Hopefully too, in examining this work readers will come to a fuller appreciation of the place of baptism in their own lives, as the writing of this work did for me.

ACKNOWLEDGEMENTS

Between the time that a thesis was defended and this book brought to completion, much has happened. I am still grateful to all those who first made this work possible: to Ephrem Carr, osb who directed me in this work, to those who helped me go to S. Anslemo, the parish of St. Charles in Edmonton, Alberta and the Oblates of Mary Immaculate, St. Mary's province, as well as the provincial and federal student loan programs. I want to thank all those who helped me while I was in Rome, especially Sharon McMillan, SND. I am especially grateful to Kenrick School of Theology in St. Louis for its generous sabbatical program that gave me the time needed to prepare this work for publication, and to the faculty, staff and students there who have been so supportive. I am grateful to Susan A. Keefe who was more than kind in sharing her work and insight with me. There is also a legion of libraries across the United States and in Rome who have shown kindness and unfailing assistance. Still it is the friends, family, colleagues and students who have made this work both possible and worthwhile. Not all of them will see this, but they all share in any contribution this book might make. As for the faults, they are mine alone.

April 5, 1998
Palm Sunday

INTRODUCTION

Agnosce, o christiane, dignitatem tuam, et *diuinæ consors factus
naturæ* (2Pt 1:4), noli in ueterem utilitatem degeneri conuersatione
recidere. Memento cuius capitis et cuius sis corporis *membrum*
(1Cor 6:15). Reminiscere quia erutus *de potestate tenebrarum,
translatus* es in Dei *lumen* et *regnum* (Col 1:13). Per baptismatis
sacramentum *Spiritus sancti* factus es *templum* (1Cor 6:19), noli
tantum habitatorem prauis de te actibus effugare et diaboli te iterum
subicere seruituti, quia *pretium* (1Cor 6:20, 7:23) tuum sanguis est
Christi, quia *in ueritate* te *iudicabit* (Ps 95:13), qui misericorditer te
redemit, Christus Dominus noster.[1]

One of the great gifts of the Second Vatican Council (1962-1965) is the
rediscovery of the centrality of Christian initiation in the life of the church. Thus
the words of pope St. Leo the Great (440-461)[2] have regained a special relevance
fifteen centuries after they were first heard. It has been in large part through the
study of documents such as this from the early and so-called 'classical'[3] eras of the

---

[1]Sermo In nativitate domini (1), *Sancti Leonis magni romani pontificis
tractatvs septem et nonaginta*, ed. A. Chavasse, CCL, vol. 138 (Turnhout:
Brepols, 1973), pp. 88-89.

[2]In this work, the years listed in brackets behind the names of rulers will be that
of the duration of their reign or, for bishops and popes, years of their ministry in
the given see. Any deviation from this pattern will be noted at that time.

[3]See B. Neunheuser, *Storia della liturgia attraverso le epoche culturali*,
Bibliotheca "Ephemerides Liturgicae," "Subsidia," vol. 11 (Rome: Centro
liturgico Vincenziano, Edizione Liturgiche, 1977), pp. 55-84; also see M. Searle,
Christening: The Making of Christians (Collegeville, MN: The Liturgical Press,
1980), pp. 10-13.

liturgy that the rediscovery of this vision of the Christian life and of the church itself has been achieved. Through such study the meaning of current rituals is being more and more deeply understood; in this same spirit, the treasury of the church's tradition is being re-examined, and much has been found which shows the continuity of vision and continued vitality of this living tradition.

One period in this history which has not been so carefully considered to this point is the time of the emperor Charlemagne (768-814). There exists a wealth of documentation from this era, and it is the goal of this study to take up one moment of this history and to submit it to closer examination. This study will focus on the letter concerning the meaning of the rites of initiation, written at the court of the emperor Charlemagne and sent to the metropolitan archbishops of his realm (hereafter referred to as the 'circular letter'[4]) and on the responses which they gave.

The date of the circular letter can be established with some certainty. There is no reason to doubt that it is a letter from the court of Charlemagne, and because of the honorific *Romanum gubernans imperium*[5] from the period after his imperial coronation in the year 800. The date can be further narrowed by internal evidence. The version addressed to Amalarius, who was then leading the church at Trier,[6] narrows the date, as he was archbishop there only from 809-814. From the

---

[4]Charlemagne made use of this literary form when he needed information from or was demanding changes in several parts of his empire at the same time. This Carolingian equivalent to the form letter was also used by the emperor in the *Epistola de litteris calendis* of 794-800 to establish schools at all of the abbeys and cathedrals of the realm. See H. Jedin, J. Dolan, F. Kempf, H.G. Beck, E. Ewig, J. Jungmann, gen. eds., *Handbook of Church History*, vol 3: *The Church in the Age of Feudalism*, trans. A. Biggs (New York: Herder, 1969), p. 85.

[5]F. Wiegand, *Erzbischof Odilbert von Mailand über die Taufe: Ein Beitrag zur Geschichte der Taufliturgie im Zeitalter Karls des Großen*, Studien zur Geschichte der Theologie und der Kirche, N. Bonwetsch, R. Seeberg, eds., vol. 4/1 (Leipzig: 1899; reprint ed., Aalen: Scientia Verlag, 1972), p. 23.

[6]*Amalarii episcopi opera liturgica omnia*, vol. 1, ed. J.M. Hanssens, StT, vol. 138 (Vatican City: Polyglott Press, 1948), pp. 235-236.

responses further data is available. Maxentius of Aquileia is one of the respondents so the date is limited by the beginning of his ministry in Aquileia in 811. Bouhot[7] narrows the date further by pointing to the mission of Amalarius to Constantinople in the spring of 813. Since the letter was answered by this time, the date generally accepted is 811/12. Thus the study of the circular letter and responses hopes to reveal a snapshot of the state of the baptismal liturgy across the empire at this single moment in time.

Even though the circular letter and responses will be the focus of this study, reference will necessarily be made to the sources upon which the metropolitan archbishops have drawn in formulating their responses. While the approach will be in the first instance historical, the theology of initiation will clearly not be avoided. Much of what is written is more than a description, it is an exposition on the meaning of the rites of initiation and on the church which celebrated them. The study of this moment in time is crucial, since it will reveal the rites of initiation on the eve of their dissolution.

The study will proceed in the following manner: first, the range of possible documents and respondents will be examined in their historical context in order to establish criteria for examining the list of documents which could be part of the response tradition. Those to be included will take two forms: 1) those which are direct responses and 2) those which are not direct responses, but seem to arise from a response which has since been lost. These texts will then be analyzed to establish models of the baptismal rituals in use at the onset of the ninth century. Finally these documents and models will be compared to examine the theological significance of each type.

---

[7]J.-P. Bouhot, "Explications du rituel baptismal à l'époque carolingienne," *Revue des études augustiniennes* 24 (1978): 285.

.

PART ONE

THE SETTING

CHAPTER ONE

THE POSSIBLE SOURCES.

The primary documents involved in this study are the circular letter of the court of Charlemagne and the responses of the metropolitan archbishops to which it was addressed. Here two difficulties arise, since it is not clear on the one hand which of the documents are actually direct responses to the circular letter, nor on the other is it clear to whom the emperor sent the circular letter. The question to be answered, then, is how many responses can be allowed, and from whom.

1. The Range of Possible Documents.

With regard to the first difficulty, there are three categories of documents which must be excluded in order to establish the list of direct responses to the emperor: a) pre-existent documents or *fontes*; b) works which arose from the process of consultation which some metropolitan archbishops undertook in preparing their responses and c) those documents which later reworked the direct responses to the emperor.

A. *Fontes*.

These are the basic documents on baptism used in the Carolingian era, for many of the respondents these are the sources used in the creation of responses to the circular letter. In this area four sources stand out:

i) The *Epistola Iohannis diaconi ad Senarium*.[1]

This work, of Roman origin, is from the sixth century. Its importance may have been increased when the author was elected as pope John I (523-526).[2] At any rate, for Dahlhaus-Berg[3] and others it is thought to have served as the base for *Primo paganus*, "a little work whose exact origin is unknown but which was very popular in ecclesiastical circles"[4] and for the circular letter itself. This theory will be examined in the course of this study.

ii) The catechesis *Primo paganus*.

This document is a description of the rites of baptism, giving a brief explanation of each element of the rite. It was used by an advisor to Charlemagne, the monk Alcuin (ca. 730-804.) He used the document in two letters,[5] and in his

---

[1]A. Wilmart, ed., *Analecta reginensia, Extraits des manuscrits Latins de la reine Christine conservés au Vatican,* StT, vol. 59 (Vatican City: Polyglott Press, 1933), pp. 170-179.

[2]See R.M. Grant, "Development of the Christian Catechumenate," in *Made, Not Born: New Perspectives on Christian Initiation and the Catechumenate,* ed. The Murphy Center for Liturgical Research (Notre Dame, IN: The University of Notre Dame Press, 1976), p. 46. This opinion is based upon the conclusion "Quant au diacre Jean...c'est-à-dire le futur pape Jean Ier." of A. Dondeyne "La discipline des scrutins dans l'église latine avant Charlemagne," *Revue d'histoire ecclésiastique* 28 (1932): 752.

[3]E. Dahlhaus-Berg, *Nova antiquitas et antiqua novitas: Typologische Exegese und isidorianisches Geschichtsbild bei Theodulf von Orléans,* Kölner historische Abhandlungen, vol. 23 (Vienna-Cologne: Böhlau, 1975), pp. 96-97.

[4]R. Cabié, *"The Sacraments,* The Church at Prayer, vol. 3, gen. ed. A.G. Martimort, trans. M.J. O'Connell (Collegeville, MN: The Liturgical Press, 1986-1988), p. 68.

[5]E. Dümmler, ed., *Epistolae karolini aevi,* vol. 2, MGH, Epistolae, vol. 4 (Berlin: Weidmann, 1895), pp. 202-203, 210-216, Alcvini epistolae 134 (the letter to Oduin) and 137 (a letter to Leidrad) [not 234 and 237 as in Cabié, "Christian Initiation," p. 68]. Both letters are from about the year 798.

De divinis officiis liber.[6] It is also used in many of the works which may have been responses to the circular letter. Keefe notes that the circular letter itself did much to boost its importance: "In fact, the popularity of 'Primo paganus' as an instruction for priests or as a model for fuller instructions was the result of Charlemagne's baptismal inquiry of 812."[7]

iii) The so called 'florilegium' on the symbolism of baptism, *De baptismi officio ac misticis sensibus eorumque auctoribus nominatim designatis et de ordine venientium ad fidem eiusdemque mysterii*.[8]

There are a number of versions of this work (texts numbered 01, 02, 03, 04 and 06 in the 'handlist' of Keefe). Odilbert of Milan (805-814) claims to have compiled the version he uses as a response to the emperor, but Keefe has shown through the use of textual criticism that he was not its compiler and further that he did not adapt it, but merely added the salutations needed to address the work to the emperor.[9] This type of work was very popular, since it ensured the orthodoxy of the work and gave the opinion of the compiler the weight of patristic authority.

---

[6]*B. Flacci Albini sive Alchuuini, Abbatis, Karoli Magni regis, ac imperatoris, Magistri: Opera quae hactenus reperiri potuerunt: Nonnulla auctius et emendatius; pleraque nunc primum ex codd. mss. edita. Accessere B. Paulini Aquileiensis Patriarchae Contra Felicem Vrgel. episc.*, ed. A. Quercetanus [Du Chesne] (Paris: S. Cramoisy, 1617), cols. 1157-1162.

[7]S.A. Keefe, "Carolingian Baptismal Expositions: A Handlist of Tracts and Manuscripts," in *Carolingian Essays: Andrew W. Mellon Lectures in Early Christian Studies*, ed. U.R. Blumenthal (Washington, D.C.: The Catholic University of America Press, 1983), p. 185, TEXT 9, note 1.

[8]Wilmart, *Analecta*, pp. 157-170.

[9]Keefe, "Handlist," p. 179, TEXT 1, note 1. Keefe has since questioned the association of this document with Odilbert. This issue will be discussed in part two.

iv) Isidore of Seville, *De Ecclesiasticis Officiis*[10] and *Etymologiarum*.[11]

The writings of Isidore were extensively used in this time,[12] especially by the compilers of the florilegia. The format of Isidore's works, a series of definitions explaining the various rites and ministries in the church, lends itself to the genre of the florilegia. In responding to the circular letter, or in creating instructions on baptism, the works of Isidore provided a clear and ordered explanation of the main moments of the initiation ritual.

All of these documents will often be cited or in some cases taken over without change in the responses of the metropolitan archbishops. This seems a natural thing to do, since it was easy and would enhance the orthodoxy of the response.

B. Consultation.

Not only did many of the metropolitan archbishops draw on already existing works in formulating their responses, but at least one, Magnus of Sens (801-818), asked his suffragans[13] and, according to Rudolf Pokorny,[14] a synod in Sens to make comments on these questions before formulating his own response to the emperor. In the case of Magnus we have a document from at least one suffragan, Theodulf of Orleans (788-821), as well as the document of a synod at

---

[10]*Sancti Isidori episcopi Hispalensis, De ecclesiasticis officiis*, ed. C. Lawson, CCL, vol. 113 (Turnhout: Brepols, 1989).

[11]*Isidori Hispalensis Episcopi etymologiarvm sive originvm, libri XX*, 2 vols., ed. W.M. Lindsay (Oxford: Clarendon Press, 1911).

[12]Of the 61 documents signaled by Keefe, 24 make major use of his works.

[13]A document of Theodulf of Orléans (*PL*, vol. 105, cols. 223-240) as well as two anonymous documents (G. Morin, "Textes inédits relatifs au symbôle et à la vie chrétienne," *RB* 22 (1905): 513-514; and an unpublished document) are all cited by Magnus in his response.

[14]See R. Pokorny, "Zur Taufumfrage Karls des Grossen," *ALW* 26 (1984): 166-173. The text in question is found in *PL*, vol. 98, cols. 939-940.

Sens, both of which exist (in the case of the synod only in a fragmentary version) in a form which addresses the questions of the circular letter, but are intended for the use of Magnus, not as direct responses to the emperor. The fact that these documents include a protocol to the emperor makes the task of discerning which are the actual responses to the circular letter more complicated.

C. Later versions.

There exists a sizable body of documents which will be called 'offspring' of the responses to the circular letter. Several suffragan bishops appear to have reused the material contained in these responses as a basis for catechetical documents to be used in their own dioceses. The number of extant manuscripts[15] of the responses of the metropolitan archbishops and other documents from suffragans (and the fact that they were copied and preserved at all) show that these documents were in wide use for a long time after 812. In cases where the original response is known, such 'offspring' documents can be set aside. However for those whose theoretical parent document is now lost, such documents, hereafter referred to as 'derivatives', form the only remaining witness to what the response contained, and so will be used as the best known version of what originally may have been a response.

Given this wealth of documentation, it is often difficult to discern which manuscripts represent actual responses to the circular letter. For this reason it is important to find out how many metropolitan archbishops existed at that time, thus giving a limit to the number of responses that can be expected.

2. The Metropolitan Sees and Archbishops.

This is the second difficulty mentioned above. The difficulty in establishing who would be the recipients of the circular letter of the emperor has been largely passed over, but it is not a simple matter for two reasons. First, the limiting of the recipients to the metropolitan archbishops is problematic, given what we know of

---

[15]See, for example, the case of Amalarius, Appendix 3, p. 179-184.

the ordering of the church in the Frankish empire at this time. Second is the question of where these metropolitan sees were, and who their archbishops were in the years 811-812.

A. The structure of ecclesiastical provinces.

Most authors,[16] in dealing with the issue of the list of potential recipients of the circular letter, refer to the "Testament of Charlemagne"[17] of 812 and the twenty-one metropolitan sees mentioned in this document. Charlemagne wills two-thirds of his wealth to be divided equally between these twenty-one sees. This presents a picture of a well-ordered church, with clearly established ecclesiastical provinces. While certain of the documents which form part of this study seem to point to such a situation in the area near the centre of the empire, for example in Sens, it seems not to have been generally the case for three reasons: i) The attitude of the emperor, ii) the evidence of Amalarius of Trier and iii) the dispute between Vienne and Arles.

i) The attitude of Charlemagne.

While the circular letter shows the emperor making use of his metropolitan archbishops, he seems to have had little use for a system of ecclesiastical provinces. Sometime between the years 786-791 Charlemagne wrote a letter concerning the nature of the Holy Spirit to five bishops, of whom only two were metropolitans.[18] If the emperor had been interested in promoting such a system of

---

[16]See Dahlhaus-Berg, *Nova Antiquitas*, p. 101; also see Bouhot, "Explications," p. 293.

[17]*Einhard: Vita Karoli magni*, ed. G. Waitz, 6th ed., MGH, Scriptores rerum Germanicarum in usum scholarum separatim editi, vol. 25 (Hanover: Hahn, 1911, reprint 1965), pp. 37-41, no. 33.

[18]J. Mabillon, *Veterum analectorum complectens varia fragmenta & epistolia scriptorum ecclesiasticorum, tam prosa, quam metro, hactenus inedita*, 4 vols. (Paris: L. Billaine/E. Martin & J. Boudot, 1675-1685) vol. 4, p. 312 (2nd ed. published in one volume as *Vetera analecta* [Paris: Montalant, 1723], p. 74): "De gratia septiformis Spiritus. Karolus divina misericordia Rex Francorum et

governance, surely he would have made use of it more often. E. Lesne, in
discussing the metropolitan system, agrees:

> Dans la pensée de Charles, l'autorité royale suffit à faire observer
> les règles de la discipline ecclésiastique. Pour ordonner et diriger
> l'Église franque, il n'a besoin, ni de l'organisation provinciale, ni du
> concours des métropolitains.[19]

The creation of the metropolitan see at Salzburg in 798 would seem to contradict
such an assertion, but Lesne rightly points out that, "Charlemagne n'eût
probablement pas songé de lui-même à instituer cette métropole, mais il a cru
politique d'accorder à l'épiscopat bavarois une satisfaction qui ne lui coûtait rien."[20]

In addition, the system of provinces established by St. Boniface (673-754)
in the re-evangelization of this area had essentially ceased to function by this time,
and thus the title of metropolitan or archbishop appears to have been a mark of
esteem bestowed by the pope, generally at the behest of the civil leaders. It was
only under the urging of the papacy and the arrival of a copy of Roman canon
law[21] that Charlemagne was moved to create a system of metropolitan archbishops

---

Langobardorum, ac Patricius Romanorum, Hiltibaldo (Coloniensi) [785-819],
Maginharto (Rotomagensi) [772-799], Agino (Bergomensi) [758-ca. 797], Geroho
(Eisterensi) [786-801], Hartricho (Tolosano) [785-791], sanctis Episcopis."

[19]E. Lesne, *La hiérarchie épiscopale: provinces, métropolitains, primats en
Gaule et Germanie depuis la réforme de saint Boniface jusqu'à la mort
d'Hincmar, 742-882*, Mémoirs et travaux des professeurs des facultés catholiques
de Lille, vol. 1 (Lille/Paris: A. Picard et fils, 1905), p. 61.

[20]Ibid., p. 67.

[21]The common form of the capitulary of Herstal, written in the year 779, canon
one, states: De metropolitanis, ut suffraganii episcopi eis secundum canones
subiecti sint, et ea quae erga ministerium illorum emendanda cognoscunt, libenti
animo emendent atque corrigant. (The Lombard form begins, "De metropolitanis
episcopis, ut *eorum* suffragani episcopi,"). A. Boretius, ed., *Capitvlaria Regvm
Francorvm*, vol. 1, MGH, Legum, Section 2, vol. 1 (Hanover: Hahn, 1883), p.
47.

12

and provinces.

ii) The evidence of Amalarius.

In the response of Amalarius of Trier to the circular letter there is a telling passage which sheds some light on this issue:

55. Dixistis, serenissime auguste, velle vos scire qualiter nos et

nostri suffraganei doceremus populum Dei de baptismi sacramento;

haec prout potuimus praelibavimus. Suffraganeus est nomen

mediae significationis; ideo nescimus quale fixum ei apponere

debeamus, aut presbiterorum, aut abbatum, aut diaconorum, aut

ceterorum graduum inferiorum. 56. Si forte episcoporum nomen,

qui aliquando vestrae civitati subiecti erant, addere debemus, oro ut

hoc non inputet dominus servo suo, quia usque in praesens tempus

non sum ausus ea adtingere quae nobis iniuncta non sunt, sed

paratus sum omnium Christi servorum vestigia sequi.[22]

For Lesne,[23] this indicates that Trier at this point is not a metropolitan see. To the current author this presents new difficulties, because it was the emperor who renewed this system of ecclesiastical governance. Surely Charlemagne knew in his own mind where the metropolitan sees were. More likely would be a scenario which would have Amalarius, relatively new to the task, having been elected in 809, honestly unaware of this aspect of his responsibilities, or else unable to assert this authority because of unwilling suffragans. Either of these seem a more plausible explanation than a ploy on the part of Amalarius to feign ignorance for whatever reason.

An alternative explanation comes from L. Duchesne, who asserts that Amalarius was not actually archbishop of Trier, but was in fact only an interim

---

[22]Hanssens, *Amalarii*, vol. 1, p. 250.

[23]Lesne, *Hiérarchie*, pp. 67-68.

administrator.[24] Knowing the power of Charlemagne it does seem unlikely that Amalarius would have attempted to deceive the emperor. Still, the theory that Amalarius had this role while being unaware of its meaning is supported by the existence of other non-metropolitan archbishops at this time, such as Theodulf of Orleans (788-821), and Angilramme of Metz (768-791), of whom Amalarius, who came from Metz, was surely aware.[25] At any rate the system of ecclesiastical provinces seems not to have been as established a reality as the 'Testament of Charlemagne' indicates.

iii) The dispute between Vienne and Arles.

Further evidence of the nebulous quality of the metropolitan system can be seen in the fact that the boundaries of ecclesiastical provinces were still unclear. The Council of Frankfurt (794) tried to deal with the ongoing boundary dispute between Vienne and Arles.[26]

It must have seemed to Charlemagne, given metropolitan archbishops of the caliber of Amalarius who were not fulfilling their role and others who were bickering over territory like worldly princes, that the whole system was more trouble than it was worth. For this study, this lack of clarity points to the difficulties in trying to establish the number of recipients of the circular letter.

---

[24]L. Duchesne, *Fastes épiscopaux de l'ancienne Gaule*, vol. 3: *Les provinces du Nord et de l'Est* (Paris: Fontemoing/E. DeBoccard, 1915), p. 41: "Cet évêque [Amalarius] est omis dans tous les anciens catalogues; seuls, les deux derniers l'admettent. Il exerça quelque temps les fonctions épiscopales à Trèves, mais non point à titre ordinaire et définitif."

[25]See Lesne, *Hiérarchie*, p. 71.

[26]See A. Werminghoff, ed., *Concilia aevi karolini*, vol. 1, MGH, Legum, Section 3: Concilia, vol. 2/1 (Hanover: Hahn, 1979), pp. 110-171, especially capitulary 8 on p. 167; also see C. de Clercq, gen. ed., *Dizionario dei concili*, 6 vols. (Vatican City: Città nuova, 1963-1967) vol. 2, pp. 86-87.

B. The 'Testament of Charlemagne'.

The 'Testament of Charlemagne' does not suffice in establishing the names of a list of recipients of the circular letter for three reasons. First, there is extant a response from Maxentius of Aquileia. Aquileia at this time is still very much a metropolitan see, and indeed a patriarchate, but it does not form part of the list in the 'Testament of Charlemagne'. This response has been linked with the presence of Frejus in the list of metropolitans. Second, two metropolitan sees from the Southwest frontier of the empire seem to be missing, Narbonne and Eauze. Third, the presence of Rome and Ravenna in this list requires special comment.

i) The question of Aquileia and Frejus.

In order to understand the question of Aquileia, a brief history is required.[27] Aquileia was considered one of the four patriarchates of the West, together with Rome, Ravenna and Milan. All four claimed apostolic origins and were from earliest times major ecclesiastical centres. But Aquileia fell on hard times and was conquered by the Lombards, forcing the patriarch to flee to the nearby island of Grado, taking with him the treasures of the church. The patriarch was established there for several years and then in Cividale to the north.

The reaction of the West to the Second Council of Constantinople (553) also figures in this history. Paulinus of Aquileia (557-569), together with his suffragans, condemned this council as being monophysite and so fell from communion. Grado, for its part, remained faithful throughout this time and was, as a reward, established as the inheritor of the patriarchal see. From 614 Epiphanius of Grado[28] and his successors claimed the title of patriarch of Aquileia.

---

[27]A more complete history, from which the following is adapted, is found in *Dictionnaire d'histoire et de géographie ecclésiastiques* s.v. "Aquilee," by P. Richard, "Grado," by S. Tramontin and "Charlemagne," by A. Dumas.

[28]However P.B. Gams, ed., *Series episcoporum ecclesiæ catholicæ* (Regensburg: G.J. Manz, 1873), lists Epiphanius as being patriarch of Aquileia (612-13). A list of two sets of claimants follows for a time until the end of the

After Aquileia re-entered communion in 700 at the council of Aquileia, there were two claimants to the same apostolic origin. The Roman solution was to acknowledge both as patriarchates. In 716 Gregory II (715-731) split the territory and Aquileia received the less important territory which was at that time outside the empire and among the barbarians, while Grado was assigned as metropolitan over that part of the empire formerly considered part of Aquileia. The two sees were often found to be usurping each other's territory. With the creation of the metropolitan see of Salzburg in 798 the area of Aquileia was further curtailed to the south bank of the Drave river. On the basis of this evidence it could be argued that Aquileia was deliberately omitted from the circle of metropolitan governance.

In the time of Charlemagne, however, two patriarchs of Aquileia figure prominently. The first is Sigwald (762-776), who assisted the emperor in the subduing of the Lombards. The second is the successor of Sigwald, Paulinus II (776-802). Paulinus was, before his election, part of the royal court and an important voice in the councils of the time.

Given this history it is impossible that Charlemagne would have ignored Aquileia. The assistance of Sigwald and the importance of Paulinus would surely have removed any doubt of the orthodoxy of the patriarchate. The prominence of these patriarchs would also preclude any forgetfulness on the part of the emperor.

A possible solution would be the precarious position of Aquileia in the empire. The territory was on the fringe of the empire, easily within the grasp of the Avars who were still a menace. It could well be that Charlemagne was not interested in having his generosity being lost to invading forces of pagan tribes of the East. On the other hand, Charlemagne had already given a substantial gift to Aquileia.[29] He may have decided that this was a sufficent legacy for the church in

schism in the year 700. Gams assigns Grado its own patriarch in 717.

[29] An order of 811 assigned to Aquileia the inheritance of two brothers which had been destined to go to Charlemagne. See E. Mühlbacher, ed., *Die Urkunden Pippins, Karlmanns und Karls des Grossen*, MGH, Diplomata Karolinorvm, vol. 1

16

Aquileia, and so left this see out of his will.

However, there is a body of opinion which holds that when Charlemagne names Frejus as a metropolitan (*Forum Iuli*) he was in fact meaning the patriarch of Aquileia. For example, R.B. De Rubeis, in editing a number of rites known as being from Frejus, claims the following:

> Scrutinia prædicta voco *Aquilejensia* aut *Forojuliensia*: ritus enim erant Ecclesiæ quæ hoc ævo dicebatur *Aquilejensis*, loco & sede *Forojuliensis*. Hoc etiam sensu inter viginti & unam Metropolitanas Ecclesias, quas suo in Testamento anni 811 beneficiis cumulavit Carolus Magnus, numerat *Forumjulium*; quo scilicet in loco, cum Aquileija excisa foret, sedem tenebant Patriarchæ. *Forojulienses* dictos in vetustis monumentis legimus *Serenum, Calistum, Paulinum*, aliosque, ad Sedis nempe locum habito respectu; simulque *Aquilejenses*, titulo scilicet, aut ipsi vocabant sese in Diplomatibus, aut eos vocabant alii.[30]

Indeed Gams lists a metropolitan of Aquileia in the year 855 as "Theutmarus (Hindelmar.) praeest synodo Ticin., 'Aquil. sive Forojuliensis

---

(Hanover: Hahn, 1906), pp. 286-287, no. 214: "Sed quia locus, in quo hoc facere optabat, admodum arctus vel strictus habebatur, ut condigne ibidem hoc facere non valeret, petiit celsitudini nostrae, ut in elemosina nostra ad eandem sanctam sedem aliquam portionem hereditatis, quam Rotgaudus Langobardus et germanus illius Felix intra civitatem vel foras prope moenia civitatis ipsius habuerunt et propter eorum infidelitatem....Nos vero de tam praeclari operis constructione exhilarati condonamus atque confirmamus supradictam portionem duorum praedictorum fratrum infidelium Rotgaudi videlicet et Felicis, quae ad ius nostrum pertinere dinoscebatur, in elemosina nostra pro mercedis animae nostrae augmento ecclesiae sanctae dei genitricis Mariae vel ad ipsam sedem Aquileiensem.... tradimus atque confirmamus et in perpetuum mansurum esse volumus."

[30]B.M. DeRubeis, *Dissertationes duae: prima de Turrianio, seu Tyrannio Rufino monacho & presbytero: altera de vetustis liturgicis aliisque sacris Ritibus, qui vigebant olim in aliquibus Forojuliensis provinciæ ecclesiis* (Venice: S. Occhi, 1754), p. 228.

patriarcha.'"[31] Still the question as to whether the sees were later known as being associated is not the essential question; what is important is to discern whether Charlemagne thought of them as separate sees. The legacy which he left to Aquileia mentions the church of the Mother of God, but this is no help, since both sees have churches dedicated to Mary. Still in the act of donation he uses the name Aquileia, and seems to indicate that the gift is to be used in Aquileia, not Frejus. That Frejus is not known a century later as a metropolitan would argue for the position of De Rubeis, still there is a hundred year period in which nothing is known of the see or its bishops. Given all the evidence, there is nothing which would exclude the possibility that both were considered metropolitans at this time.

ii) The sees on the Spanish frontier.

Two sees in the area of the empire which bordered on the Spanish frontier are not mentioned in the 'Testament of Charlemagne,' but for diverse reasons.

a) Eauze.

This metropolitan see, once facing the Atlantic on the coast of what is now Southern France, has a large lacuna in its history which corresponds to the time we are studying. From the years 673/680 until 879 there is no reference to this metropolitan see or any archbishop in refuge claiming Eauze as his see. When the see, but not the town, reappears in 879 it is in the nearby town of Auch. The best that can be discerned is that this seaside town was destroyed by Scandinavian pirates and not rebuilt until the early tenth century when references to Eauze reappear. At any rate, it is unlikely that Charlemagne would have included this see in his will. It is not even certain that such a see existed at this time. The responsibilities for this province seem to have been taken over for a time by the neighboring province of Bordeaux, for which there is also no firm list of archbishops at this time. It may well be that the see established at Auch had not yet have taken on the duties of a metropolitan see, since the town of Auch will not

---

[31]Gams, ed., *Series episcoporum*, p. 773.

18

be documented as the replacement metropolitan for another sixty years. It seems unlikely that the circular letter would have been sent by the emperor or have been received by any theoretical metropolitan archbishop of this ecclesiastical province, let alone an answer sent in this era.

b) Narbonne.

This metropolitan see was on the opposite side of what is now the South of France, and looked out on the Mediterranean. The town was of crucial strategic importance for the Frankish empire and the Saracens, each of whom used it as a base for operations against the other. So while it was held tenaciously, it was in continual danger of being overrun. This could explain its absence from the 'Testament of Charlemagne', for the same reason as Aquileia. Surely the emperor would not have wanted to add to the treasury of the Saracens. Still, given the existence of a response from Aquileia we cannot discount the possibility that Narbonne, like the patriarchate, received the circular letter. Gros holds that an ancient hispanic ritual which was in place until the early ninth century can be discerned:

> El estudio de los Ordinarios - Rituales y Pontificales - catalanes y
> narbonenses que se conservan nos ha llevado a identificar dos ordos
> bautismales que, según se deduce de su contenido y de su estado de
> evolución, nos permiten reconstruir con bastante exactitud el
> primitivo rito bautismal que a principios del siglo IX, en los
> obispados de la antigua metrópoli de Narbona, vino a sustituir el
> ordo bautismal hispánico.[32]

However it is precisely at the time of the circular letter that the change to a more Roman baptismal *ordo* took place under the influence of Benedict of Aniane, partly in reaction to the adoptionist controversy:

---

[32]See M.S. Gros, "El antiguo ordo bautismal catalano-narbonense," *Hispania sacra* 28 (1975): 37.

La crisi adopcionista y la reforma promovida por Benito de Aniana
fueron ciertamente la causas de este cambio, y todo parece indicar
que el arzobispo Nebridio fue quien la llevó a término. Por todo
ello, con mucha razón, podemos considerar el ordo bautismal
catalano-narbonese como un texto elaborado en torno al año 800,
poco después que Nebridio fuese nombrado arzobispo de
Narbona.[33]

Given the attention that Nimfridius apparently paid to baptism, a response from
Narbonne may be among the anonymous documents, but because of the changes
which happened during his ministry, such a response may be without any
specifically Iberian features to mark it out as the response of the metropolitan.

The name of the metropolitan archbishop at this time is Nimfridius, which
begins with the letter 'N', the letter found at the point of address in one form of the
circular letter, extant in two manuscripts, but this is almost certainly a reference to
the place where the *nomen* of the recipient would go.[34]

iii) Rome and Ravenna.

Whether Rome received the circular letter is a question with no easy
answer. Whether it is possible to extrapolate the concept of the emperor's
authority over Rome and his understanding of the pope as one who was under the
emperor's protection into the sending of the circular letter is conjecture. It would
have been the height of presumption for the emperor to suggest that he was
responsible for the ordering of the liturgy in the churches of Rome; on the other
hand, the emperor created and held his empire by asserting his authority not only
over princes, but also bishops and popes. At any rate, we can judge the likelihood

---

[33]Ibid., p. 78.

[34]According to Keefe, "Handlist," pp. 189 and 190, TEXT 14, note 4, the
manuscripts involved are Vienna, Österreichische Nationalbibliothek lat. 398
(twelfth century) and Zwettl, Stiftsbibliothek 283 (thirteenth century).

of the response which would arise from any such act. Simply put, there is no way that Rome would have even acknowledged receipt of the circular letter. While the papacy was not at a particularly high point in its history, it surely would not allow itself to be instructed on matters of the liturgy by the emperor.

The exarchate of Ravenna had its own peculiar circumstances. 'Liberated' by Charlemagne from the Lombards, it was given, however reluctantly, to Rome as part of the so-called 'Patrimony of St. Peter'.[35] As a patriarchate and a former political power in the early days of the Constantinople-based empire, it had no inclinations of subservience to either Rome or Aachen and tended to pit one against the other. As part of the papal states, it could escape the rule of Charlemagne,[36] while on the other hand it could confront the papacy: "...even in the exarchate the pope had to meet the challenge of the archbishop of Ravenna, whose strivings for autonomy had Charles's support."[37] In this light it would be difficult to postulate a response to the circular letter from the patriarch of

---

[35]Based upon the forged *Donation of Constantine*: "Unde ut non pontificalis apex 17. vilescat, sed magis amplius quam terreni imperii dignitas et gloriae potentia decoretur, ecce tam palatium nostrum, ut praelatum est, quamque Romae urbis et omnes Italiae seu occidentalium regionum provincias, loca et civitates saepefato beatissimo pontifici, patri nostro Silvestrio, universali papae, contradentes atque relinquentes eius vel successorum ipsius pontificum potestati et ditioni firma imperiali censura per hanc nostram divalem sacram et pragmaticum constitutum decernimus disponenda atque iuri sanctae Romanae ecclesiae concedimus permanenda." *Das Constitutum Constantini (Konstantinische Schenkung): Text,* ed. H. Fuhrmann, MGH, Fontes Iuris Germanici Antiqui, in usum scholarum, vol. 10 (Hanover: Hahn, 1968), pp. 93-94. This division was reaffirmed by Adrian I and Charlemagne according to the "Vita Hadriani Papae I." See Mansi, *Sacrorum conciliorum nova, et amplissima collectio,* 53 vols. (Florence/Venice: 1759-1798, facsimile reproduction Arnheim/Paris/Leipzig: H. Welter, 1901-1927), vol. 12, cols. 737-738.

[36]Ravenna is not part of the reform councils of the empire in May and June of 813; see Werminghoff, *Concilia aevi karolini,* vol. 1, pp. 245-306.

[37]G. Barraclough, *The Medieval Papacy,* Library of European Civilization (London: Thames and Hudson, 1968 and 1979), p. 44.

Ravenna. Thus these two metropolitan sees can be removed from the list of expected responses to the circular letter. This places the total back at twenty-one metropolitan sees, but it changes the geographic picture considerably.

The result of this historical investigation is a list of between twenty-two and twenty-four (depending on the existence of Eauze/Auch and the status of Frejus) metropolitan sees of which twenty or twenty-one could have received and responded to the circular letter. Definite names exist for seventeen of the metropolitan archbishops, for two more there are possible names and two, Bordeaux and Frejus, have left not even the name of the bishop to history.

Table 1 on the following page gives a roster of those metropolitan archbishops under Frankish protection at the time in question, together with their years of ministry in that see, the name of their see as they would have known it as well as the name of the city as it is known today.[38] Only those who may have received and responded to the circular letter are included, so Eauze, Rome and Ravenna are excluded.

---

[38]The information on the names and the years of ministry of the archbishops is taken from Gams, ed., *Series episcoporum.*

TABLE 1

POSSIBLE METROPOLITAN ARCHBISHOP RECIPIENTS
OF THE CIRCULAR LETTER

ANCIENT NAME	TODAY'S NAME	ARCHBISHOP IN 811/812
AQUILEIA	AQUILEIA	MAXENTIUS (811-833)
ARELATE/ARELAS	ARLES	JOHN II (811-819)
BITURIGIS	BOURGES	EBROINUS (810-pre 820)
BURDEGALA	BORDEAUX	UNKNOWN
COLONIA	COLOGNE	HILDEBALD/HILDEBRAND (785-819)
DARANTASIA/ TARANTASIA	MOUTIERS EN TARENTAISE	RADABERTUS (post 800-pre 828)
EBRODUNUM	EMBRUN	(Marcellus? Bernard?)
FORUM IULII	FREJUS	UNKNOWN
GRADUS	GRADO	(John?)
LUNGDUNUM	LYONS	LEIDRAD (798-814)
MEDIOLANUM	MILAN	ODILBERT (805-814)
MORGONTIACUS	MAINZ	RICULF (787-813)
NARBO(NA)	NARBONNE	NIMFRIDIUS (799-post 822)
REMIS	RHEIMS	VULFARIUS (808-816)
ROTOMAGNUS	ROUEN	GILBERT (?800-828)
SALISBURGENSIS	SALZBURG	ARNO (785-821)
SENONES	SENS	MAGNUS (801-818)
TREVERISIS	TRIER	AMALARIUS (809-814)
TURONES	TOURS	JOSEPH (802-813)
VESONTIO	BESANCON	BEROIN (811-829)
VIENNA	VIENNE	S. BERNARD (808/10-842)

CHAPTER TWO

THE HISTORICAL SETTING

In order to better understand the significance of the documents, it is important to situate them historically. Three aspects of life in the empire will be considered to demonstrate the setting in which the circular letter was delivered. The purpose is to try to discern something about the mind of the emperor who sent the circular letter. The three aspects are: i) the situation of the emperor and his family; ii) a brief addition to what has been said concerning the situation of the local churches in the empire; and iii) the relationship between the emperor and the popes who ministered during his reign. With this understanding of the person of the emperor, the place which the liturgy and especially baptism held in the empire can then be considered.

1. The Emperor and His Family.

First we must consider Charlemagne himself, at the age of seventy and near the end of his lengthy reign. His lifetime has seen the re-birth of culture in the Frankish lands, and the court at Aachen has been at the centre of this renaissance. Charlemagne, though he never learned to write, had composed poetry[1] and been concerned with the importance of education as no Frankish king before him. He is, however, clearly aware that the end is near; he has written his last will and testament and will be dead in less than two years. He is evidently in poor health, judging from the protestations to the contrary which will be seen in the responses to the circular letter. On the other hand he is still, with his son, the unquestioned

---

[1]See, for example, E. Dümmler, ed., *Poetae Latini aevi Carolini*, vol. 1, MGH, Poetarvm Latinorvm medii aevi, vol. 1 (Berlin: Weidmann, 1881), p. 90.

ruler of his empire.

The reign has not been an easy one. The emperor has spent much of his time fighting battles, early on with the Lombards, later with the Avars, the Saxons and the Nordic tribes and almost continually with the Saracens who threatened the empire from their Iberian base.

He had felt a sense of religious obligation and power to some degree all through his reign. This becomes clear in analyzing the salutation given at the beginning of his letters over the course of his reign. The early letters are marked by a very brief salutation, "Carolus gratia dei rex Francorum vir illuster."[2] Starting in the Fall of 774 *et Langobardorum* is inserted before *vir illuster*, and there is an increasingly common addition *ac Patricius Romanorum*. It was the grace of God that had made him king and Roman patrician, and it was his responsibility to use his reign for the furthering of God's will. The next stage of this development begins to surface in May of 801, some time after his coronation by pope Leo III (795-816). As Dumas notes:

> Pourtant Charlemagne ne se prévalut pas immédiatement du titre impérial. Dans un diplôme du 4 mars 801 il s'en tenait encore au titre de patrice des Romains....Au bout de quelques mois les hésitations de Charlemagne cessèrent. Laissant tomber son titre de patrice, il se dit officiellement empereur. C'est ce qui apparaît dans un diplôme du 29 mai 801. Désormais, jusqu'à sa mort, il s'intitula dans ses actes: Karolus, serenissimus Augustus a Deo coronatus, magnus, pacificus imperator, Romanum gubernans imperium, qui et

---

[2]E. Mühlbacher, *Diplomata Karolinorvm*, vol. 1, p. 81. *Illuster* is a form peculiar to Charlemagne of *illustris*. Thus C. DuCange, *Glossarium mediae et infimae Latinitatis*, with supplement by D.P. Carpenter and G. Henschel, New Edition, L. Favre, (ed.), vol. 4 (Graz, Austria, Akademischen Druck U. Verlagsanstalt, 1954), p. 294 "Exhinc Reges alii Franciae, indeque Majores domus, qui Regulorum vices obtinebant, *Illustris* nomenclaturam servarunt, aut sibi arrogarunt."

per misericordiam Dei rex Francorum atque Langobardorum.[3]
This is a radical change which indicates a new understanding of the emperor as the
instrument of God. This salutation is more than just a form of diplomatic
language, it is a statement of fact. The citation shows the person speaking was
crowned by God. For Barraclough and especially Wallace-Hadrill[4] this is also seen
in the coronation of Christmas day 800; it was the active role that the pope took in
the ceremony that offended Charlemagne, not the giving of the title itself. For the
emperor there was no need for an intermediary at his coronation. Many of the
documents from this time onwards begin with "In nomine patris et filii et spiritus
sancti,"[5] further indicating that what follows is spoken in the name of the Trinity.

But the future of the Carolingian line which had seemed so secure with
three sons already crowned as kings over a part of the empire was suddenly shaken
to its foundations with the death of one son, Pepin, in July of 810 and then of a
second, Charles, in December of 811. Just as Charlemagne himself and his brother
Carloman had inherited the realm of their father, the empire had been divided
between his three sons; and just as Carloman did not endure as king, so the line of
Charlemagne's sons would be tragically reduced to a single heir. These
experiences must have produced a profoundly changed monarch. "It was
salvation," according to J. Wallace-Hadrill, "that the emperor was concerned
about, his own and his people's."[6] Only one legitimate heir, who will be known as

---

[3]*Dictionnaire d'histoire et de géographie ecclésiastiques*, s.v. "Charlemagne,"
by A. Dumas, col. 439.

[4]Barraclough, *Medieval Papacy*, pp. 54-55; Wallace-Hadrill, *The Frankish
Church*, pp. 188-189. See also Jedin, Dolan, Kempf, Beck, Ewig, Jungmann,
gen. eds., *Handbook of Church History*, vol 3, pp. 93-94.

[5]Mühlbacher, *Diplomata Karolinorvm*, vol. 1, p. 276.

[6]J.M. Wallace-Hadrill, *The Frankish Church*, Oxford History of the Christian
Church, H. Chadwick, O. Chadwick, eds., vol. 3 (Oxford: Clarendon Press,
1983), p. 190.

Louis the Pious (813-840), remains and so is to be crowned co-emperor within months and heir to the title of emperor, which had been destined to die with Charlemagne. With the loss of these sons and other members of his family and court, coupled with his own failing health, it is natural that his thoughts would have turned to matters of salvation.

To complete the picture, W. Ohnsorge points to a further development of the title, "The last form of Charles' imperial title, dating from the year 813, used only the expression 'Imperator et Augustus' before 'Rex Francorum et Langobardorum.'"[7]

As for the internal governance of the empire, the civil strife which will follow the death of Charlemagne is kept at bay, but only while the emperor lives. A power struggle will begin shortly after his death, pitting Louis against his own son Lothar I (817-844). This will continue in the line of rulers which follows until 887 when the empire which Charlemagne had won during his turbulent life is dismembered. One wonders if the emperor had a sense of the trouble coming to his beloved empire.

2. The Local Churches in the Empire.

The setting of the church at this time is also one of controlled instability. Charlemagne will, until his last days, be occupied with reform councils, ever trying to maintain order and orthodoxy within the church, among its bishops and in its liturgy.[8] The place of the bishop as servant of God, realized in service to the emperor, has been established in no small part by the efforts of Alcuin who had trained many of the metropolitans when they were students at the palace school;

---

[7]W. Ohnsorge, "The Coronation and Byzantium," in *The Coronation of Charlemagne: What Did It Signify?*, ed. and trans. R.E. Sullivan, Problems in European Civilization, vol. 3 (Boston: Heath, 1959), p. 90.

[8]Reform councils were held in Arles, Rheims, Mainz, Chalons-sur-Saôn and Tours in May and June of 813, only a few months before the emperor's death. See Werminghoff, *Concilia aevi karolini*, vol. 1, pp. 245-306.

but the organization of ecclesiastical provinces has not gone smoothly: bickering between metropolitan sees has been frequent, and the faith, which was so much a part of all of Charlemagne's battles and conquests, is still easily swayed, especially among the first generation Christians in some of the newly acquired or re-acquired areas: "The most urgent need in many parts of the Frankish lands at the end of the eighth century appears to have been, after all, to impose any sort of Christian ritual at all."[9] Even with these difficulties of basic faith and ecclesiastic administration, they are the emperor's bishops: they are appointed at his behest, are summoned by him to councils and exhorted by him in letters. They may receive the pallium from Rome, but it is always at the request of the emperor. And when the emperor dies their influence and often their ministry came to an end.

Much has been made of the so-called 'Romanizing' tendencies of the emperor with reference to the introduction of the Roman liturgy into the realm:

La nouveauté réside dans le fait que, depuis la seconde moitié du VIIIe siècle, la monarchie franque emploiera l'authorité dont elle dispose pour promouvoir officellement l'établissement du cérémonial romain et pour évincer, par le fait même, l'ancienne liturgie autochtone, dite gallicane.[10]

---

[9]R. McKitterick, *The Frankish Church and the Carolingian Reforms, 789-895*, Royal Historical Society Studies in History, vol. 2 (London: Royal Historical Society, 1977), p. 119.

[10]C. Vogel, "La réforme liturgique sous Charlemagne," in *Karl der Grosse: Lebenswerk und Nachleben*, gen. ed. W. Braunfels, 5 vols. (Düsseldorf: L. Schwann, 1965-1968), vol. 2: *Das geistige Leben*, ed. B. Bischoff, p. 217. This position has long been held, for example J. Mabillon, *De liturgia Gallicana, libri III* (Paris: E. Martin and J. Boudot, 1685), p. 16: "Ordinem Romanum...receptus est in Gallia vigere coepisse jam inde a tempore Caroli M. sive id effecerint Romani Pontifices, qui alias omnes ecclesias ad unum cum Romana concentum, quantum in eis fuit, adducere curarunt: sive ad eos demerendos id voluerit Carolus."

Certainly there is some truth in this assertion: the *Hadrianum*,[11] the sacramentary sent by pope Adrian I (772-795) to Charlemagne, has spread throughout the realm. Likewise for the sacrament of baptism there is some evidence that Roman practice was at the heart of the early attempts by Charlemagne to reform this sacrament. In the *Duplex legislationis edictum*, from the year 789, canon 23 states, "Ut audiant episcopi baptisterium presbyterorum, ut secundum morem Romanum baptizent."[12] The term *morem (mos)* may indicate *law*, but equally has the meaning of *custom* or *usage*.

There needs to be, however, a more nuanced understanding of this Romanization, particularly after the year 800. Judging from textual evidence, especially in what has been seen in the letters of the emperor, three important facts become clear: i) Charlemagne saw himself as the instrument of God, having won a Christian empire, ii) related to this, he saw it as his role to direct the ecclesiastical authorities in his realm, preferably with as little reference as possible to the bishops of Rome, for whom he had limited respect and iii) the emphasis he placed upon education and *scriptoria* led to the spread of the liturgy as much as anything he

---

[11]See J. Deshusses, ed., *Le sacramentaire grégorien: Ses principales formes d'après les plus anciens manuscrits*, 3 vols., comparative ed., 2nd ed., revised and corrected, Spicilegium Friburgense, vol. 16 (Fribourg: Editions Fribourg Suisse, 1979), vol. 1, *Le Sacramentaire, le supplément d'Aniane* (hereafter *Hadrianum*).

[12]Boretius, ed., *Capitvlaria Regvm Francorvm*, vol. 1, p. 64. Vogel, in "Réform liturgique," p. 221 is partially in error when he says, "Un Capitulaire de 769 environ, reprenant un décret donné en 742 par Carloman, institue un examen pour les curés...sur le baptème, le symbole....Le concile de Neuching (772) précise que l'évêque devra s'assurer si les prêtres soumis à leur juridiction prêchent et administrent les sacrements conformément à la tradition romaine. The council of Neuching deals with the ministry of monks in parish life, and does not speak of the Roman tradition. The canon (no. 5 of the year 742) is essentially identical to that from 769 (canon no. 6): "Decrevimus, ut secundum canones unusquisque episcopus in sua parrochia sollicitudinem adhibeat, adiuvante gravione qui defensor ecclesiae est, ut populus Dei paganias non faciat...." From Boretius, *Capitvlaria Regvm Francorvm*, vol. 1, p. 25 and p. 45. The regulation does resurface at the reform council of Mainz in 813.

himself enacted.[13]

Charlemagne saw it as his divinely instituted role to maintain order in the Church:

> Charles's conception of his position in the church left scarcely more
> room than that of emperors such as Justinian for an independent
> papacy. Charles had no doubt about his vocation. Like
> Constantine the Great and his successors, he regarded himself as
> guardian of the faith - even against the pope, if need be - and lord
> over the church. He it was whom (in Alcuin's words) 'the
> dispensation of our Lord Jesus has made rector of the Christian
> people'; on him rested 'the whole salvation' - note the word 'whole'!
> - 'of the Church of Christ.'[14]

And it is not only those in the royal court who saw this ordering of the universe; the greetings to Charlemagne in the protocol of each of the responses to the circular letter are equally clear on the understanding of the place of the archbishop under the emperor. This is implicitly clear in the fact that they would respond at all to a circular letter on liturgical matters, but there is further evidence in the responses themselves. The protocol from the response of Amalarius of Trier shows this clearly:

> GLORIOSISSIMO ET EXCELLENTISSIMO AUGUSTO A DEO
> CORONATO KAROLO SERENISSIMO VITA SALUSQUE

---

[13]See C. De Clercq, *La législation religeuse franque de Clovis à Charlemagne (507-814)*, Recueil de travaux publiés par les membres des Conférences d'Histoire et de Philologie, series 2, vol. 38 (Paris: Bureaux du Recueil Bibliothèque de l'Université and Louvain: Librarie du Recueil Sirey, S.A., 1936), pp. 181-182: "Cette multiplication des manuscrits liturgiques a contribué à la diffusion du rite romain en Gaule bien plus que n'importe quel acte officiel: on ne connaît d'ailleurs acune texte législatif imposant cette transformation, sauf le voeu de Charlemagne concernant la romanisation du rituel du baptême."

[14]Baraclough, *Medieval Papacy*, pp. 44-45.

PERPETUA.

1. Domine mi, christianissime imperator, misistis ad servulum vestrum inquisitiones secundum vestram misericordiam de sacro baptismate....Quamquam idoneus non sim vestrae interrogationi respondere, *tamen inobedientem me non oportet esse* [emphasis mine], nisi omnibus sensibus et intellectu meo vestris sanctis iussionibus obtemperem.[15]

While others are not so effusive in their praise of the emperor, all acknowledge the fact that he has the right to control the church and its liturgy (note the term *inobedientem* above), and that not answering the questions of the emperor concerning the liturgy would be equivalent to treason.

The bishops who receive the letter are, for the most part, well into their ministry, and within two years about one-third of the sees will have new metropolitan archbishops. Some, such as Amalarius, have done much to advance the spirituality of the church, while others, such as Magnus of Sens, have well-organized ecclesiastical provinces. Still the local church appears to see itself as an instrument of the emperor, who was in turn the instrument of God and able to call each of his servants to account for the use of the power and privileges which they have been given.

3. The Relationship Between the Emperor and the Popes.

The link between the church of Rome and the empire has become more and more tentative with the passage of the years; the ceremonies of Christmas day 800 seem to have marked the beginning of the end for this relationship which neither side seems to have understood fully and which had been a common means to competing ends.

This is seen first of all in the fact that the claim to the imperial title of the West is being established through direct diplomacy with the emperor of the East

---

[15]Hanssens, *Amalarii*, vol. 1, pp. 236-237.

Nicephorus (802-811)[16] so that when Charlemagne died, he was universally recognized as emperor of the West, successor to the line of Constantine and the Caesars, without needing to rely on the papacy or Constantinople to affirm this title:

> ...in 813 he viewed his emperorship as a sovereign expression of
> power, which the holder, following Charles' example, could in the
> future give over to his successor without calling upon papal
> cooperation or without getting recognition from the East, but solely
> out of his own fulness of power.[17]

A second aspect is that while in the early days he may have appeared to be trying to be servant to the tradition of Rome, at this point in time such a role would not fit with the data. Again Dumas:

> Non content de diriger l'Église franque, Charlemagne prétendit
> aussi s'imposer au Souverain pontife. Assurément il ne cessa de
> proclamer son respect pour le Siège apostolique. Mais, maître de

---

[16]Achieved in 811 according to G.H. Pertz, F. Kurze, eds., *Annales fuldenses sive Annales regni Francorum orientalis ab Einhardo, Ruodolfo, Meginhardo fuldensibus, Seligenstadi, Fuldae, Mogontiaci consripti cum continuationibus ratisbonensi et altahensibus*, MGH, Scriptores rerum Germanicarum in usum scholarum separatim editi, vol. 7 (Hanover: Hahn, 1891), p. 19: "Qui legatos Karli ad Niciforum missos Constantinopoli audivit et absolvit; cum quibus et suos legatos direxit et pacem a Niciforo incoeptam confirmavit. Qui etiam, ubi ad imperatorem Aquisgrani venerunt, scriptum pacti ab eo in ecclesia sucipientes more suo, id est graeca lingua, laudes ei dixerunt, imperatorem eum et basileum appelantes." Ohnsorge, in "The Coronation and Byzantium," p. 89, speaks of the same event as happening in 812, "The result was that Constantinople decided in 812 to make a virtue of necessity, and through an official act the Byzantine legate in Aachen recognized Charles as the spiritual 'brother' of the Byzantines and of the emperor-basileus instead of the previously used 'son' - he is the 'emperor of the Franks,' as [the Byzantine historian] Theophanes says....Thus Byzantium had in no way departed from its ideology; it had merely introduced into the order of its designations for crowned rulers under the world emperor in Constantinople a special designation for the Frankish King."

[17]Ohnsorge, "The Coronation and Byzantium," p. 90.

32

Rome comme *patricius Romanorum*, il tend de plus en plus à
traiter le pape en subordonné.[18]

Indeed, in his final testament Rome is apportioned only one of the twenty-one shares of the gift which Charlemagne leaves the church. From the text it appears that he even expected Rome to share this gift with its suffragan sees, just like any other metropolitan. The greetings which the emperor sent to pope Leo III (795-816) at his election show rather clearly the understanding of the relationship between the empire and the church, and are worth quoting:

> Nostrum est: secundum auxilium divinae pietatis sanctam undique
> Christi ecclesiam ab incursu paganorum et ab infidelium
> devastatione armis defendere foris, et intus catholicae fidei
> agnitione munire. Vestrum est, sanctissime pater: elevatis ad
> Deum cum Moyse manibus nostram adiuvare militiam, quatenus
> vobis intercedentibus Deo ductore et datore populus christianus
> super inimicos sui sancti nominis ubique semper habeat victoriam,
> et nomen domini nostri Iesu Christi toto clarificetur in orbe.
> Vestrae vero auctoritatis prudentia canonicis ubique inhereat
> sanctionibus et sanctorum statuta patrum semper sequatur;
> quatenus totius sanctitatis exempla omnibus evidenter in vestra
> fulgeant conversatione, et sanctae admonitionis exhortatio audiatur
> ab ore; quantenus luceat lux vestra coram hominibus, ut videant
> opera vestra bona et glorificent patrem vestrum, qui in caelis est.[19]

From this text it would seem that he was ruler not only in the Roman church but of the Roman church. As protector of the holy shrines of the apostles Peter and Paul in the City and holder of the keys to the shrine of the Holy

---

[18]*Dictionnaire d'histoire et de géographie ecclésiastiques*, s.v. "Charlemagne," by A. Dumas, col. 436.

[19]Dümmler, *Epistolae karolini aevi*, vol. 2, pp. 137-138.

Sepulchre,[20] there was sufficient prompting for the emperor to think and act autonomously, to accept direction only from God.

The way in which Louis the Pious was crowned on September 11, 813, shows this same sense of overlordship. It is the coronation liturgy that points to the understanding of what this really means, and in a ceremony which must have been truly moving for its simplicity we have a real example of *legem credendi lex statuat supplicandi*:[21] the emperor *shows* what is being handed on to his son.

According to one account the crowning was done, not by Charlemagne, and not by the pope, but by Louis himself. The crown was placed on the altar of the palace chapel in Aachen by Charlemagne, and, after he and Louis prostrated themselves before the altar in prayer, Louis was instructed to place the crown on his own head.[22] The reality expressed is that the co-emperor was crowned directly by God, not by the pope, nor even, in this account, by Charlemagne. The location of the ceremony, in the palace chapel at Aachen, also points this out and was a conscious choice, for it was the centre from which Charlemagne had discerned God's will and acted upon it.

> En sa simplicité, la scène d'Aix-la-Chapelle dépasse en importance
> celle qui s'était déroulée à Saint-Pierre de Rome le jour de Noël de

---

[20]See G.H. Pertz, F. Kurze, eds., *Annales regni Francorum inde ab a. 741 usque ad a. 829 qui dicuntur Annales laurissenses maiores et Einhardi*, MGH, Scriptores rerum Germanicarum in usum scholarum separatim editi, vol. 6 (Hanover: Hahn, 1895), p. 108: "Eodem anno [799] monachus quidam de Hierosolimis veniens benedictionem et reliquias de sepulchro Domini, quos patriarcha Hierosolimitanus domno regi miserat detulit. Azan praefectus civitatis quae dicitur Osca, claves urbis per legatum suum cum muneribus transmisit."

[21]From the "Capitula Celestina," see J. Mansi, *Sacrorum Conciliorum*, vol. 4, col. 461; also H. Denzinger, A. Schönmetzer, eds., *Enchiridion symbolorum, definitionum et declarationum de rebus fidei et morum*, 35th ed., emended (Freiburg in Breisgau: Herder, 1973), p. 91, no. 246.

[22]This according to J. Wallace-Hadrill, *The Frankish Church*, p. 189; G. Barraclough, *The Medieval Papacy*, p. 55, has Charlemagne placing the crown on Louis' head. In either case it is not the pope.

34

l'an 800. Quelle qu'eût été alors la part faite à Charlemagne dans

l'organisation de la cérémonie, celle-ci ne laissait pas de donner à

l'Église et à son représentantur un rôle dès plus voyants; à Aix, la

cérémonie est religiuese, mais elle demeure toute laïque. C'est du

pape Léon que Charlemagne avait reçu la couronne; c'est de la

volonté de Charles que Louis tient la sienne.[23]

Louis will crown Lothar I in this same place in 817.

The evidence found in the circular letter and the responses seems to
indicate that at this point in his life Charlemagne, though still interested in the state
of the liturgy in his empire, was not insisting upon a slavish following of Roman
usages. There is no mention of Rome or its liturgy in the circular letter, nor are
the metropolitan sees called to follow Rome in all things. This is shown in the fact
that the question of the laying on of the hand, a practice of the Roman church,
does not enter the circular letter. Rather, the concern of the emperor is orthodoxy
and the agreement between what is taught and what is done.

From this briefest glance at the evidence, any assumption that Charlemagne
was attempting at this point to Romanize the liturgy of Christian initiation,
particularly with regard to specific rites within the ritual, will have to be held in
great suspicion.

4. The Place of Liturgy and Baptism in the Empire.

From the foregoing what can be concluded about the place of the liturgy in
the Frankish realm and why should it be of great interest to the emperor? "This
was a subject upon which his views were decided and obstinate," remarks Gregory
Dix, "His orderly mind was offended as much by the ceremonial and liturgical
diversity of the churches in his dominions as by the disorder and disorganization of

---

[23]E. Amann, *L'epoque carolinienne*, Histoire de l'Église depuis les origines
jusqu'a nos jours, A. Fliche, V. Martin, eds., vol. 6 (St. Dizier: Blond & Gay,
1937), pp. 186-187.

episcopal administration which were its underlying cause."[24] According to Dix and
a host of others Charlemagne understood that the liturgy expressed the state of the
church in the realm. As the liturgy went, so went the church, and as the church
appeared, so appeared the empire. Thus the linkage with Rome in the earlier part
of his reign and the later insistence of this era on careful celebration and the unity
between belief and actions show that there is this motive behind the desire for a
unified liturgy and that Charlemagne was indeed much more than "an autocrat with
a hobby."[25]

In the early part of his reign the emperor had a program of making
Christians of the peoples which he conquered. "Thus military occupation and
forced conversion went hand in hand."[26] This is particularly the case among the
Saxons: "His [Widukind of the Saxons] people were submitted to draconian
measures of control...."[27] Still there is a development in this policy, probably
because it simply did not work:

> To us it seems obvious that Christianity thus imposed could only
> lead to further rebellion - which indeed is what happened. To
> Charlemagne and his advisors things looked otherwise. Only a few
> voices were raised in warning, Alcuin's among them. After a
> further decade of revolts and suppressions a milder capitulary was
> promulgated in 797.[28]

From a liturgical perspective, a careful analysis of the documentation of the
Gallican liturgy shows that the rites of baptism had been in a serious state of

---

[24]G. Dix, *The Shape of the Liturgy*, 2nd ed. (London: A & C Black, 1945;
Seabury ed., San Francisco: Harper & Row, 1982), p. 575.

[25]Ibid., p. 575.

[26]J. Wallace-Hadrill, *The Frankish Church*, p. 183.

[27]Ibid.

[28]Ibid., p. 183-184.

36

decline. The series of rites and instructions which had been the rites of the catechumenate had all but disappeared; in the *Missale Bobbiense* the rites *Ad Christianum faciendum*, which, according to Duchesne is the traditional term for the start of the catechumenate,[29] survive only as part of the Easter Vigil liturgy or for baptism *in extremis*.[30]

The case of baptism had one feature which was especially important. The heart of the baptismal rite for Charlemagne was the creed or symbol. It was the symbol of the faith and its understanding by the faithful that was foremost in the emperor's mind, as it was this element that he asked to have introduced in the

---

[29]L. Duchesne, *Origines du culte Chrétien: Etude sur la liturgie latine avant Charlemagne* (Paris: E. Thorin, 1889), p. 281: "les rites qui consacraient l'entrée du converti dans cette catégorie inférieure portent, dans les vieux livres liturgiques, la rubrique *ad christianum faciendum*, ou un autre du même sens."

[30]See E.A. Lowe, ed., *The Bobbio Missal: A Gallican Mass-Book (MS. Paris Lat. 13246)*, The Henry Bradshaw Society, vol. 58 (London: Harrison & Sons, 1920), pp. 71-72, nos. 228-233. This terminology is found in the *Gelasianum* and in two forms in several of the so-called 'Gelasian sacramentaries of the eighth century'. It is often the title of the sections used for baptism *in extremis*. In the other cases the terminology is associated with rites of the catechumenate, but is usually placed between the scrutinies and the blessing of the font. For the first type see: L.C. Mohlberg, L. Eizenhöfer, P. Siffrin, eds., *Liber sacramentorum romanae aeclesiae ordinis anni circuli (Cod. Vat. Reg. lat. 316/Paris Bibl. Nat. 7193, 41/56) (Sacramentarium Gelasianum)*, Rerum ecclesiasticarum documenta, Series maior, Fontes, vol. 4, 3rd ed. (Rome: Herder, 1981), p. 93, no. 598; P. Saint-Roche, ed., *Liber Sacramentorum Engolismensis*, CCL, vol. 169C (Turnhout: Brepols, 1987), p. 295, no. 1990: Item ad Caticuminum ex pagano faciendum; A. Dumas ed., *Liber Sacramentorum Gellonensis*, CCL, vol. 159 (Turnhout: Brepols, 1981), p. 339, section 345, no. 2344: Ordo ad infirmum caticuminum faciendum sive baptizandum; for the second type see A. Hänggi, A. Schönherr, eds., *Sacramentarium Rhenaugiense*, Spicilegium Friburgense, vol. 15 (Freibourg, Switzerland: Universitätsverlag, 1970), p. 232, no. 159 and *Engolismensis*, p. 95, no. 686: Orationes super electos ad caticuminum faciendum. These eighth century Gelasians are all from the last half of the eighth century. The placement of this terminology for the ordinary ritual and its use for baptism *in extremis* may be remnants of the collapse of a fuller ritual, first to a single celebration for those in danger of death and then to a single celebration as the usual form of the ritual.

Eucharistic liturgy in his empire. Right words, orthodoxy, this was the clearest outward sign of the unity of the Christian empire he had built, as Keefe observes:

> The rite of baptism, comprising the entire initiation process for a
> Christian from catechetical preparation to reception of the
> Eucharist as a full member of the Church, put its stamp on every
> individual not only as part of the Church, but as a member of
> society. It was often the only thing that distinguished the peoples
> of the newly conquered borders of the Carolingian empire from the
> pagan tribes.[31]

Alongside of this lies the line of thought which would link this concern with a sense of history. As he had studied some history, he was surely aware that the symbol of faith was at the centre of the great controversy which the emperor Constantine (312-337) had to settle at the council of Nicea (325). Could it be that Charlemagne is here trying to style himself along the lines of this model of Christian emperors? Certainly ideas such as these were not uncommon in the empire.[32] Or perhaps he is simply trying to avoid the difficulties which had plagued his ancestor to the imperial throne. Whatever the reason, for Charlemagne the importance of baptism stems from the symbol of faith contained therein, and from this one faith flowed the unified liturgy, the sign of the unity of the empire.

---

[31]Keefe, "Handlist," p. 171. Also M. Navoni, "Dai Longobardi ai Carolingi," in A. Caprioli, A. Rimolai, L. Vaccaro, eds., Storia Religiosa della Lombardia, *Diocesi di Milano*, vol. 1 (Brescia: Editrice 'La Scuola', 1990) p. 101: "...sorretto dalla persuasione che soltatnto un cristiano fedele alle rinunce e alle promesse battesimali potesse essere, per coerenza, anche un buon cittadino, secondo la tipica visione medievale della *societas christiana* dove i valori religiosi e civili si fondonoe si identificano, trovando nel sacramento del battesimo la loro origine e nel battistero il loro segno distintivo."

[32]See, for example, the letter of Hadrian I from 778, no. 60 in the 'Codex Carolinus,' Societas Aperiendis Fontibus Rerum Germanicarum Medii Aevi, ed., *Epistolae Merowingici et Karolini aevi*, vol. 1, MGH, Epistolarum, vol. 3 (Berlin: Weidmann, 1892), pp. 586-587.

38

Finally it must be noted that the importance of baptism was also seen in a catechetical light. For those who were sponsors or parents, the baptismal liturgy told them as much about themselves as about the person being baptized. Again from Keefe,

> There is another way that baptism, as a rite, was the cornerstone of Carolingian society. In its preparatory stages, whether for adult catechumens or sponsors of infant candidates, baptism was an opportunity for education.[33]

This, in the opinion of Keefe, is the reason for the circular letter. J. Lynch writes extensively of the important role of the godparent in society and the liturgy. The godparent becomes:

> ...the primary nonclerical participant in a baptism, eventually ousting parents from every liturgical act. In a paradoxical way, the sponsor even came to overshadow the infant being baptized....the Carolingian church succeeded in recreating a function for the baptismal liturgy, recasting the services to educate, test, and impress the godparents, who in turn were entrusted with the future religious formation of their godchildren.[34]

Whatever the exact moment of motivation, it is clear that the emperor saw his empire as a Christian empire and understood initiation into the faith as expressing the meaning of membership in this society, entrusted to his leadership by God. Thus he was willing to spend considerable time and what was left of his failing health to ensure that this moment in the lives of his people was rightly understood and taught by the leaders of his church. This is clear from the text of the circular letter and was surely not lost on the metropolitan archbishops who

---

[33]Keefe, "Handlist," p. 171.

[34]J.H. Lynch, *Godparents and Kinship in Early Medieval Europe* (Princeton, NJ: Princeton University Press, 1986), p. 297.

responded to it. What we are dealing with, then, in turning to the circular letter and responses is a matter of central import to Charlemagne and his subjects: the place of the faith in this Christian empire.

PART TWO

ANALYSIS

CHAPTER THREE

THE INDIVIDUAL TEXTS

1. The Studies of the Texts.

A. An overview of the literature.

While there has been no comparative analysis of the texts of the circular letter and known responses, this does not mean that the area of Carolingian baptismal works has not been examined. Apart from the individual editions of the circular letter and several of the known actual or possible responses, there have been a number of works which have attempted to inventory the known documents. Four such efforts are worthy of note, as they will figure more or less prominently in the chapters which follow.

The first of these four comes from 1927 in the form of an article by Hanssens,[1] who, in publishing two anonymous documents, placed them in the broader context of the circular letter. Hanssens signaled the circular letter and responses from five known authors and five anonymous works which seemed to be responses to the circular letter. A second effort, the 1975 study of Dahlhaus-Berg,[2] gave the same results. A third more expanded version was the work of

---

[1] J.M. Hanssens, "Deux documents carolingiens sur le baptême," *EL* 41 (1927): 69-82.

[2] Dahlhaus-Berg, *Nova Antiquitas*, pp. 99-108.

42

Bouhot,[3] who in 1978 brought together references of a broader range of documents on the subject of baptism in the Carolingian era. Among the references in this work are the same five responses of known authorship, an additional anonymous response giving six, to three of which authors were more or less certainly assigned.

    B. The work of Keefe.

Finally in 1983 came the work of Keefe, "Carolingian Baptismal Expositions: A Handlist of Tracts and Manuscripts,"[4] which brings together references to sixty-one documents and to over one hundred manuscripts. While many do not fit the scope of the current study, either in time or genre, the list has been chosen as the basic reference from which the citations in the following chapters will be made.

The choice to follow the list developed by Keefe is made for three reasons: 1) While this study is more limited in its scope, the organization of the documents by geographic area will prove most useful in the comparison of works and discerning the 'offspring' texts; 2) While it is to be checked against other works, the 'handlist' of Keefe provides the most complete organization of the material to date; and 3) For those who wish to pursue the study of Carolingian baptismal documents, this will allow for a method of cross reference, and will avoid the creation of another set of numbers and references. The list must be used with care, however, as it is not always fully consistent with data derived from other scholarly work.

The first task will be to examine this extensive list of known documents and establish, where possible, which ones are actual or possible responses to the circular letter. The documents will be referred to by their 'text' number as assigned by Keefe, and so will be noted as K01, K02, etc. The circular letter, which itself is

---

[3]Bouhot, "Explications," pp. 278-301.

[4]Keefe, "Handlist," pp. 169-237.

listed as K14 will be examined first, both because the life of Charlemagne has already been examined but also in order to establish the base of comparison for the other texts.

2. Criteria for Evaluating the Documents.

In examining the list of sixty-one documents, it is clear that not all of them are responses to the circular letter. It is important to establish criteria for discerning which texts belong to the list of responses and which do not. The exclusion from or inclusion in a list of possible responses to the circular letter will be based upon four basic criteria: a) content; b) form; c) geography; and d) salutation.

A. Content.

First is the need for the document to address the questions asked. The content needs to have a certain correlation with the circular letter. Those which, in the main, do not address the questions of the emperor will be excluded. This criterion cannot, however, be pushed too far; none of the complete responses to the circular letter, even those which doubtless are responses, follow this order exactly.

B. Form.

The document must have a format which shows it to be a response to specific questions, and not some other literary form. For this reason those which are glosses on the prayers of the rite as well as those in the form of sacerdotal examinations can be excluded, as they were written with a different purpose in mind.

C. Geography.

Third, the number of possible responses is limited to the number of possible recipients of the circular letter. Surely no two will come from the same see, and those which have the name of a metropolitan archbishop securely attached will be considered over anonymous documents from the same ecclesiastical province.

44

This use of this criterion will help discern 'offspring' and collaborative documents from the direct responses to the emperor.

D. Salutation.

Fourth, the document should have a protocol and eschatacol addressed to the emperor. This requirement will distinguish those which are direct responses from those which are 'offspring'. Still care must be taken, since there exist letters addressed to the emperor which are in fact suggestions of how to respond, written either by suffragan bishops or, in at least one case, a synod.[5]

Documents which seem to fall into the category of responses to the circular letter or 'derivatives' (offspring documents for which no source or parent response is known) will be described in terms of their author (where known), the sources used by the author and how it corresponds to the circular letter. A list of the manuscript tradition and published editions of these documents is found at the end of this work.[6] In the description of manuscripts and editions, the work of Keefe is the base, however the works of Hanssens, Dahlhaus-Berg and Bouhot mentioned above will serve as checks, in addition to the research of the current author.

Those which are 'offspring' of an extant response and those which are surely not responses will be dealt with only in proving their place outside the scope of this study.

3. K14: The Circular Letter Of Charlemagne.

Three complete versions of the text of the circular letter (K14) are extant:[7] one addressed to Amalarius of Trier, one to Odilbert of Milan, and one to

---

[5]See Pokorny, "Taufumfrage," p. 168.

[6]See Appendix 3, p.173-186.

[7]Mansi, *Sacrorum conciliorum*, vol. 17/2 col. 483, note 1, seems to signal the existence of three others, "Similes Epistolas direxit Karolus Magnus ad Joannem, Archiepiscopum Arelatensem; ad Leidradum, Archiepiscopum Lugdunensem; ad Magnum, Archiepisocpum Senonensem. Illas hîc referre perquam inutile foret; eas legere poterit Lector curiosus in *Mabillon. Analect. tom. 1. pag. 25, & tom. 3.*

an unknown recipient, 'N.' Keefe notes that this version, "...is part of a collection of form letters of Udalric of Bamberg...."[8] The citation, 'N.' is either a reference to Nimfridius of Narbonne or more likely a signal to insert the *nomen* of the recipient. The three letters are almost identical[9] and, except for the question on ceremonial breathing which is found in two forms, can be dealt with as a unity.

In addition Keefe signals a modified version of the circular letter[10] which was addressed to the priests of the diocese of Liège probably by its bishop Waltcaud (810-833). The version, according to Keefe, while certainly a form of the letter, is substantially amended, presumably to match the local situation, and so is not considered among the versions of the letter.

A. Sources used by the author.

The text of the circular letter appears to have been developed from the baptismal practice known at the royal court. Bouhot, like most scholars, holds: "Les questions, qui se rapportent à la catéchèse plutôt qu'à l'exécution des rites,

---

pag. i." But upon consultation with that work, it becomes clear that such is not the case, "Sirmundus in Notis ad Theodulfi librum superius laudatum duo potissimum observat, unum, ex quatuor hujus libri exemplaribus, quae in manus ipsius venerant, tria esse quae ad Magnum Episcopum missum doceant librum, Vindunense, Divionense et Vaticanum: at quartum Corbeïense pro Magno Joannem habere, sed mendose, uti opinatur. Verum pace optimi viri existimo nullum esse mendum. Nam cum epistola Caroli universis Galliae Episcopis transmissa fuerit, non mirum, si ex variis ejus exemplis, unum Magno Senonensi, alterum Joanni Arelatensi Archiepiscopis inscripta sint." (Mabillon, *Veterum Analectorum*, First edition, vol. 1, p. 24, rev. ed., p. 76.) The reference to Leidrad seems to spring from the existence of the response from this metropolitan in volume three of Mabillon's work

[8]Keefe, "Handlist," p. 190, TEXT 14, note 4.

[9]See Appendix 1, pp. 166-168 for a comparison of the editions of the three versions.

[10]Edition by A. Werminghoff in *Neues Archiv der Gesellscheft für altere deutsche Geschichtskunde* 27 (1902): 578-580.

46

sont inspirées par le commentaire *Primo paganus*."[11] While the circular letter has certain textual similarities with *Primo paganus*, the order of questions is different from the ordering in that work.[12] The circular letter places the scrutiny before the section on the symbol, and the sections on the exsufflation, exorcism and the giving of salt after the section on the symbol. In *Primo paganus* the scrutiny is placed after the exorcisms and *traditio symboli*, immediately before the rites of touching the nostrils and the anointings. While conventional wisdom holds the circular letter to be based directly upon the earlier document, this evidence suggests otherwise. There are two additional reasons for holding this position.

i) The person who compiled the series of questions for the emperor was not Alcuin of York, who had died in 804. The liturgy he is describing seems to have more stages than that of the circular letter, with the time of scrutiny starting after the initial renunciation and exorcism, not contemporaneously with it.

ii) The textual similarities, which amount to the name of the ceremony and occasionally a verb describing the rite, seem insufficient to establish that the circular letter is directly copied from or based upon *Primo paganus*. Since both are involved in describing baptismal rites, an absence of this resemblance would be more striking.

B. Content.

After the salutation Charlemagne explains that he is making the inquiry, not because of any heresy, but rather with the goal of focusing attention upon the baptismal liturgy so that it may be even more carefully carried out. There is no direct reference to, nor do the questions follow exactly the order of the liturgy as

---

[11]Bouhot, "Explications," p. 286.

[12]See Appendix 2, p. 169-171.

seen in the Roman baptismal *ordo* (Andrieu *Ordo XI*)[13] which has a much more complicated ritual and a different ordering of those elements it has in common with the circular letter. This would be somewhat unusual if it had been legislated as a sort of *editio typica*, thus adding weight to the argument that the term *morem* meant *custom* in the citation from the council of Mainz in 813.

The questions which follow are very precise. Charlemagne does not conceal his wish to know exactly what is going on and tries to leave no room for his metropolitan archbishops to avoid the issues at hand. He very clearly goes through a celebration of the sacrament item by item and expects the metropolitan archbishops to do likewise: "haec omnia subtili indagine per scripta nobis, sicut diximus nuntiare satage, vel, si ita teneas et praedices, aut si in hoc quod praedicas, te ipsum custodias."[14] The emperor asks one or more specific question on each moment of the ritual as he knew it, with the two rather surprising omissions of the water rite and the laying on of the hand of the bishop. From the response of Odilbert of Milan,[15] who does everything but give his opinion and who uses an already extant work of unassailable orthodoxy adding only the appropriate protocol and eschatacol for the emperor, it is clear that the royal name evokes caution and that Charlemagne is still in control of his church. The metropolitan archbishops knew they had to respond and yet were not sure how best to appease this request. That the letter is even necessary shows further that there existed

---

[13]M. Andrieu, *Les ordines romani du haut moyen âge*, 5 vols., Spicilegium Sacrum Lovaniense, Études et documents, vols. 11, 23, 24, 28 and 29 (Louvain: Spicilegium Sacrum Lovaniense, 1931-1961), vol. 2, *Les textes (ordines I-XIII)*, pp. 417-447. This *ordo* is found in both collection A and B of Andrieu, and was written at the end of the sixth or beginning of the seventh century (Andrieu, *Ordines*, vol. 2, p. 413). The *ordo* focuses more on the catechumenate than the rites of baptism.

[14]Keefe, "An Unknown Response From the Archiepiscopal Province of Sens to Charlemagne's Circulatory Inquiry on Baptism," *RB* 96 (1986): 89, lines 35-37.

[15]See the discussion of Text K01, p. 52.

considerable diversity in the forms of celebration and likely a certain laxness in the education of clergy and laity alike.

C. The individual questions.

There are eighteen questions in the circular letter. However, in asserting this number of questions, two previous studies must also be acknowledged, those of Hanssens[16] and Morin,[17] which in trying to establish the number of questions, arrive at different solutions. Hanssens finds only sixteen questions by uniting the question regarding the renunciation of Satan with that on the pomps and works of Satan and by uniting the anointing with Chrism and the use of the Chrismal veil. The text of the circular letter would indicate this to be a logical division, but since some of the metropolitan archbishops dealt with these questions separately they will be treated as separate questions in this study. Morin, in examining the letter of a work known to him as pseudo-Amalarius, shows that the author considers the introductory clause as a question and then unites not only the questions on the renunciation of Satan, but also the questions on insufflation and exorcism as well as those on the touching of the nose and the anointing of the chest and back, and then the questions on the anointing with Chrism and the Chrismal veil, thus arriving at thirteen questions. Both of these authors were citing the circular letter in terms of the manuscripts they were publishing, and so such a complete separation of the questions as is here proposed was not needed. In the case of this study, given the diversity of responses taken up in this study, a more complete separation of the questions is required. In fact, one of the questions should be broken down still further, that of the ceremonial breathing.

This question appears to have had at least two different versions from very

---

[16]Hanssens, "Deux documents," pp. 74-75.

[17]G. Morin, "Note sur une lettre attribuée faussement à Amalaire de Trèves dans le manuscrit lat. 21568 de Munich," *RB* 13 (1896): 292.

early on.[18] Some documents use the term *exsufflatio* while others have *insufflatio* and, in one case, both.[19] Another document,[20] one of those which cites the full text of the questions being asked before giving the appropriate responses, keeps *insufflatio* in the question while responding in terms of *exsufflatio*. While a detailed analysis of the responses will be the focus of the final section of this work, at this point it can at least be said that there may be in these different terms a clue to the origin of a given work. Bragança holds, in discussing a wider range of baptismal documents, that:

> La plupart des manuscrits au Nord de la Loire, emploient le mot
> *exsufflare*, qui est celui des sources romaines et de l'*Ordo L*, tandis
> que les documents du Sud, sauf quelques exceptions, utilisent le
> verb *insufflare*, comme dans la liturgie mozarabe et gallicane.[21]

The meaning of the question appears to have been equally unclear, since while most responses are in terms of breathing on the person being baptized, the document mentioned above responds in terms of the breathing on the person and on the water.

There are many currents intersecting in both the circular letter and the responses. Some respondents will volunteer information not asked for and a few even more interestingly quote questions which are not in the extant versions of the circular letter. Still, the letter seems to have come to us essentially as it left the court at Aachen in 811/812. Variants on these eighteen questions will indicate local variations. These will be dealt with as they arise.

---

[18]See Appendix 1, p. 167.

[19]A. Wilmart, ed.(posth.), "Une Catéchèse baptismale du IXe siècle," *RB* 57 (1947): 199.

[20]G. Morin, "Textes inédits," *RB* 22 (1905): 513.

[21]J. O. Bragança, "Le symbolisme des rites baptismaux au Moyen Age," *Didaskalia* 3 (1973): 45.

Table 2 on the following page lays out the questions and assigns numbers to them which will be used in this work.

TABLE 2[22]

THE QUESTIONS OF THE CIRCULAR LETTER

Question Number	Latin Text
01	Cur primo infans catecuminus efficiatur?
02	Quid sit catecuminus?
03	De scrutinio, quid sit scrutinium?
04	De symbolo, quae sit eius interpretatio secundum latinos?
05	De credulitate, quomodo credendum sit in Deum Patrem omnipotentem, et in Iesum Christum Filium eius natum et passum, et in Spiritum Sanctum, sanctam ecclesiam catholicam, et cetera que secuntur in eodem symbolo?
06	De abrenuntiatione satanae et de omnibus operibus eius atque pompis, quid sit abrenuntiatio?
07	Quae opera diaboli et pompae?
08	Cur exsuffletur?
09	Cur exorcizetur?
10	Cur catecuminus accipiat salem?
11	Quare tangantur nares?
12	Quare pectus ungatur oleo?
13	Cur scapulae signentur?
14	Quare pectus et scapulae liniantur?
15	Cur albis induitur vestimentis?
16	Cur sacro chrismate caput perunguitur?
17	Cur mystico tegitur velamine?
18	Cur corpore et sanguine dominico confirmatur?

[22]Based on Hanssens, *Amalarii*, vol. 1, pp. 235-236.

4. The Responses.

In the following discussion of the responses, a new section, marked by a capital letter will begin with each certain response or derivative document. Those texts which fall outside this study will be examined in a separate paragraph at the end of these sections.

A. Text K01: The response of Odilbert of Milan (805-814).

There are several florilegia which come from the area of Northern Italy in this era (texts 01 - 04 and 06 in the 'handlist' of Keefe), and it is one of these which has been attributed as the response of Odilbert, who used it without any adaptation[23] in his response to the emperor.

---

[23]Keefe, "Handlist," p. 179, TEXT 1, note 1. While it has been shown that the florilegium used by Odilbert of Milan in his response to the circular letter was not an original work, Keefe has further challenged the attribution of this florilegium as the response of Odilbert. [See S.A. Keefe, "The Claim of Authorship in Carolingian Baptismal Expositions: The Case of Odilbert of Milan," in *Fälschungen im Mittelalter: Internationaler Kongreß der Monumenta Germaniae Historica, München, 16.-19. September 1986*, MGH, Schriften, vol. 33/5, *Fingierte Briefe Frömmigkeit und Fälschung Realienfälschungen* (Hanover: Hahn, 1988), pp. 385-401.]
Setting aside the arguments concerning the original authorship of the document, Keefe's argument for not considering this text as a response are that it: "does not relate in any remote way to Charlemagne's questionnaire: it does not describe the way baptism was celebrated in Milan, as Charlemagne requested; nor, like the extant responses, does it describe the Roman ordo of baptism Charlemagne favored or correspond to his series of questions." (p. 391) Additional reasons for excluding it are, again according to Keefe, "its extreme brevity and use of *et cetera.*" (p. 391) These challenges will be taken up in turn.
The first question is whether the florilegium describes the Milanese liturgy. There are two points of contention. The first concerns the rites of the catechumenate, which in the twelfth century description of Beroldus, included rites which are not discussed in the florilegium. There are bodies of opinion which hold that these rites are alluded to in this document, so it is at least possible that a reference is made. The second, more important point of contention concerns the washing of the feet at the end of the ceremony. Several authors have held that the reference at the end of this text to bare feet is in fact a reference to the washing of the feet (For example, T. Schäfer, *Die Fusswaschung im monastischen Brauchtum*

und in der Lateinischen Liturgie: Liturgiegeschichtliche Untersuchung, Texte
und Arbeiten, 1. Abteilung, vol. 47 (Beuron: Beuroner Kunstverlag, 1956), pp.
16-17: Bei Johannes Diaconus ist der Sinn klar: Die Katechumenen müssen sich
barfuß den Exorcismen unterziehen....Odilbert schiebt sie jedoch ganz an den
Schluß, nach Taufe, Firmung und Eucharistie. Das ist sicher kein Zufall....Er
nimmt lieber die Autorität des Römers Johannes oder des fränkischen Florilegiums
zu Hilfe. Freilich findet sich dort kein Kapitel über die Fußwaschung; so benutzt
er das daran anklingende Kapitel von der Barfüßigkeit und stellt es ans Ende aller
Zeremonien." This argument is essentially the same as that of P.F. Beatrice in *La
lavanda dei piedi: contributo alla storia delle antiche liturgie Cristiane*,
Bibliotheca "Ephemerides Liturgicae," "Subsidia," vol. 28 (Rome: Centro
liturgico Vincenziano, Edizione Liturgiche, 1983), p. 218.), Keefe, however
disagrees, "But since John's reference to the catechumens taking off their shoes as
they approach the font has nothing to do with a foot-washing ceremony, probably
the chapter *De pedum nuditate* from John was placed last simply not to disrupt the
liturgical sequence of the revisionist." (Keefe, "The Claim of Authorship," p. 394.)

This argument tries to make a distinction between liturgical and practical
actions, but can such a distinction be made? While the act was practical, it also
had a symbolic dimension, and formed part of the liturgical action. Further the
placement of an act concerning the catechumenate after the rites of baptism would
be strange, but not if it was in fact being used in a different sense, that is as a
reference to footwashing. Using a specific reading of the liturgical data as a basis
for excluding the document as a response thus seems less than sure.

In fact to make such passing references to these rites seems more likely,
since, as Keefe herself notes (pp. 392-393, note 25) the emperor had first hand
experience of the Milanese baptismal liturgy, having his own daughter baptized by
the patriarch Thomas (759-783) in Milan in 771 (See Pertz, Kurze, eds., *Annales
regni Francorum Inde ab a. 741 usque ad A. 829*, p. 56: "[781] DCCLXXI. Et
inde revertente domno Carolo rege, Mediolanis civitate pervenit, et ibi baptizata
est filia eius domna Gisola ab archiepiscopo nomine Thoma, qui et ipse eam a
sacro baptismo manibus suscepit.") The passage of some forty years may have
dulled Charlemagne's memory as to details, but a detailed description of the ritual
would surely not have been necessary.

The second and third issues can be taken together: they deal with the
difference between the document and the form of the circular letter and the fact
that the document does not describe the Roman liturgy. Table 4 on pages 102-109
show these to be of no consequence, given the variety seen in these responses,
even those which surely are responses to the circular letter.

Further is the assertion that the text is considered to be too brief to be a
response. While responses such as that of Leidrad of Lyons are very long indeed,
others are considerably shorter than this document.

Finally the use of the term *et cetera* indicates, for Keefe, an unacceptable

54

i) The Author: Odilbert of Milan.

Little is know of Odilbert, but much is attributed to him. His nine year
ministry as patricarch of Milan saw changes in the spiritual life of his diocese:
"...sotto il cui episcopato l'abbazia di S. Ambrogio si sviluppò ulteriormente come
centro di vita spirituale per l'intera città."[24] To Odilbert are also attributed some
of the developments of the Ambrosian Eucharist and the catechesis on the
Eucharist, "...la *Exposition Missae canonicae* secondo il rito ambrosiano, che fa
parte della silloge di carattere liturgico pastorale ad uso del clero ambrosiano nel
sec. XII."[25] An important actor in the church in Milan, he resisted many
Romanizing tendencies of the culture around him.

ii) Sources used by the author.

As the name indicates, a florilegium is a gathering of texts from a number
of authors to place them together so that, according to Odilbert, "quae velut
mirificis floribus ex nimio rutilat ornata flagranti odore...."[26] So this text on
baptism is a series of citations: of the letter of John the Deacon (12 citations),
Isidore of Seville *De ecclesiasticis officiis* (11 citations) and *Etymologiarum* (2

---

use of language in a response to the emperor. However, again from documents
which are unquestionably responses we see these words, for example at the end of
the list of the works of Satan in the response of Leidrad of Lyons (see *PL*, vol. 99,
col. 859) and in Magnus of Sens' description of the symbol (see Keefe, "An
Unknown Response," p. 57, line 39.), as well as the words *et reliqua* in the
response of Amalarius of Trier in citing scripture and a list of vices (See Hanssens,
Amalarii, vol. 1, p. 239, line 8; p. 245, line 25.) Clearly, such terminology is
acceptable in citing well known sources, even in responses to the emperor. They
are surely more common in this document, but that is only because a greater use is
made of well known citations. Given all this, the document need not be exculeded
from being considered as the response of Odilbert of Milan.

[24]M. Navoni, "Dai Longobardi ai Carolingi," p.101.

[25]A. Majo, *Storia della chiesa ambrosiana: Dalle origini ai nostri giorni*
(Milian: Nuove Edizioni Duomo, 1995), p. 96.

[26]Wiegand, *Erzbischof Odilbert*, p. 27.

citations), Ambrose *De Mysteriis* (5 citations) and *De Sacramentis* (2 citations), Augustine (3 citations), Pope Gregory the Great (3 citations) and Cyprian (3 citations), one citation each from Pope Celestine and Nicetas of Remesiana, the last uncredited, three citations from the Gospels and one from 'Solomon' meaning the book of Ecclesiasticus.

iii) Content.

The text claims to be a response to Charlemagne, but the answers do not correspond exactly to the circular letter. This is not too surprising, since it uses a pre-existent document. The text begins with the biblical warrant for baptism and a discussion of the meaning of the word 'baptism' and the essence of the sacrament. Then follows the discussion of the rites, including a section on "sufflatione et exsufflatione."[27] After the section on first Eucharist are two sections which add to the questions of the circular letter, one on the laying on of the hand of the bishop and one on the need for bare feet in baptism. In summary fashion we have the following ordering of responses: The scriptural warrant of baptism, the etymology of the word *baptism*, the essence of baptism in water and word, circular letter question[28] 2, 9, 8, 10, questions on *conpetentes*, 3, catechesis with the laying on of the hand, 4 and the *traditio symboli*, a question on touching with spittle, touching the ears, the *effeta*, 11, 12, 13, 6, 1, a question on triple immersion with the invocation of the Trinity, 16, 17, 15, 18, questions on the laying on of the hand by the bishop which bestows the Holy Spirit and finally a section on bare feet.

Although the order of the questions is considerably altered, it becomes clear why Odilbert used this particular florilegium as his response to the emperor, since it covers most of the questions asked. The last item, "De pedum nuditate,"[29]

[27]Ibid., p. 29.

[28]The numbers are those assigned in Table 2, page 51. They will be used throughout the remainder of this work.

[29]Wiegand, *Erzbischof Odilbert*, p. 37.

56

likely refers to the continuation of the practice of the washing of the feet of the newly baptized which was observed in the patriarchate of Milan.

iv) Excluded documents.

Texts K02, K03, K04 and K06 are variants of text K01, and so are not part of this study.

B. Text K05: Anonymous.

Keefe assigns the origin of this document to the group of documents from Northern Italy or Switzerland,[30] an area from which a number of responses are missing. However, as it is without the protocol and eschatacol, it is not an original response, but most likely a derivative document. To this point no edition of this document has been published.[31]

i) Sources used by the author.

This document is noteworthy for, having no citation of *Primo paganus*. The text makes use of other sources, including three passages from Isidore, one concerning the meaning of the word catechumen, one concerning the writing of the symbol in the heart of the believer and a third concerning the use of salt. Six scriptural references, taken from both testaments, make up much of the rest of the document, including references for Chrismation, which is associated with the woman who anointed the feet of Jesus (Jn 12:1-8). Even though Isidore is the only patristic source cited, the document need not have been from a place in the Spanish orbit; Isidore is seen in many of the documents and may have been the only resource available to the drafter of this document.

---

[30]See Keefe, "Handlist," p. 178-184.

[31]The author is grateful to S.A. Keefe for the use of her editions of this document as well as texts K51, 52, 55, and 57, all of which are soon to be published in volume two of her work, *Water and the Word: Baptism and the Education of the Clergy in the Carolingian Empire: A Study of Texts and Manuscripts*, University of Notre Dame Press, forthcoming, 1998.

ii) Content.

The text lacks any salutation, and simply begins with the first question concerning why infants are made catechumens. This is the only question cited by the text, and according to the unpublished edition of Keefe is "cur caticuminus infans efficitur," as opposed to the question of the circular letter, "cur primo infans catecuminus efficitur."[32] The response then goes on to answer the questions in the identical order of the circular letter with the following exceptions: a) the question on the content of the symbol, the heart of the circular letter, is omitted; b) the questions on exorcism and exsufflation are treated as a unity; c) the question on the touching of the nose includes touching of the ears and mouth with saliva and d) the Chrismal veil is not mentioned.

Thus the response takes on the following form: Questions 1, 2 with catechesis, 3, 4, 6, 7, 9 and 8, 10, 11 (also touching the ears with the *effeta*, both touchings with spittle), 12 and 13, 14, 15, 16, 18. Given the almost perfect citation of the first question, the absence of the mention of the water rite and the order of the rites in the response, this document almost certainly springs from the response tradition, and from a place where the baptismal liturgy was celebrated in a very similar fashion to Aachen.

iii) Excluded documents.

Texts K07 and K08 can be excluded from this discussion. Neither addresses itself to the questions of the circular letter and in fact text K08 is merely an extended quotation from Isidore. Text K09 is surely not one of the responses, since it is quoted by Alcuin.[33] Still, it deserves mention, as this is the text *Primo paganus*, which figures so prominently in many of the works which fall within the range of the current study.

---

[32]Keefe, "An Unknown Response," p. 88, lines 20-21.

[33]Dümmler, *Epistolae karolini aevi*, vol. 2, pp. 202-203.

C. Text K10: Anonymous.

This is an anonymous work which could be a derivitive of one of the responses to the circular letter. The first line, "Cur infans caticuminus efficitur et quid sit caticuminus,"[34] is, as in text K05, almost identical to the first question in the circular letter. Like text K08, its place of origin in Northern Italy or Switzerland does not pose a barrier to its being a direct response to the circular letter. It does, however, lack the protocol and eschatacol, and so must be considered a derivative document.

i) Sources used by the author.

The two main sources used in this text are Isidore (*De ecclesiasticis officiis* Book 2, 21:1-4, 23:2-5, 24:1-2) and *Primo paganus*. Isidore is cited extensively (numbers 1, 3-4, 6-10 in the edition of Wilmart), while *Primo paganus* is used in two parts (numbers 5 and 11 in Wilmart). In addition the letter of John the Deacon is the source in altered form for the question on the exsufflation (number 2 in Wilmart).

ii) Content.

The text is a series of descriptions concerning the rites which follows the questions of the circular letter quite closely, except for moving the lengthy discussion of the symbol of faith to a later point in the response and adding points on the triple immersion and the laying on of the hand. The order in relation to the questions of the circular letter is as follows: 1 and 2, 8, 9, 10, a long section answering 4, explaining its origins with the apostles and the use of symbols or standards in wars as the model for the *traditio symboli*, 5, 3, 11, 12 in the sign of the cross, 13, 14, the water rite with three immersions, 15, 16 and 17, 18, the laying on of the hand by the bishop giving the sevenfold spirit. While it has much in common with many of the other responses in terms of sources, there is no other document which makes this particular union of Isidore and *Primo paganus*.

---

[34]Wilmart, *Analecta*, p. 166.

iii) Excluded document.

Text K11 does not fall within the scope of this study, since as a set of glosses on certain of the prayers of the ritual it does not meet the requirements of structure and content needed for consideration as a response.

D. Text K12: Anonymous.

This text is often found with text K11. It is in a question and response format, appears to answer the questions of the circular letter, and is not associated with an ecclesiastical province for which a response is extant. However because of the lack of a salutation to the emperor, it must also be considered with the derivative documents. There is an abundance of manuscripts of this document,[35] as it was incorporated into the *Pontificale romano germanico.*[36]

i) Sources used by the author.

This text makes extensive use of *Primo paganus*, citing it ten times throughout the document. Not all of the response comes from this source, however, with a substantial part coming from the hand of the author, oftentimes reusing themes common with Isidore, including that of the salt of wisdom.

ii) Content.

The text answers the questions of the circular letter as follows: 3, 2, 8, 10, 9, 10(again), 11 (including the touching of the ears, and both ears and nose touched with spittle), 13, 14, 12 (these last two are signings with the cross), 13, 14, *traditio symboli*, 6, the etymology of the word *baptism*, the water rite with a Trinitarian reference, 15, 16 and 17, 18, the laying on of the hand by the bishop for the gift of the Spirit. The content is sufficiently close to be a derivative of a response to the circular letter.

---

[35]See Appendix 3, pp. 179-181

[36]C. Vogel, R. Elze (eds.), *Le Pontifical romano-germanique du Xe siècle*, 3 vols, StT vols. 226, 227, 229 (Vatican City: Polyglott Press, 1963, 1972).

iii) Excluded document and the circular letter.

Text K13 is, according to Keefe, a series of excerpts from Isidore which do not cover the range of questions of the circular letter, and so can be excluded from this study. Text K14 is the circular letter.

E. Text K15: The response of Magnus of Sens (801-818).

i) The Author: Magnus.

Of Magnus very little is known. At one point he fulfilled the role of chaplain to Charlemagne, and throughout his career is known to have been a prolific writer. In addition, given the evidence of this study, it seems that Magnus was a competent administrator and author, a worthy bishop who was not known for much else besides his service to his church.

ii) Sources used by the author.

The protocol of the letter of Magnus explains how this response was formulated, "Gloriosissime imperator, innotescere magnitudini vestrae praesumpsimus nos servi vestri, Magnus scilicet et ceteri compares mei, licet indigni episcopi ad Senonicam dioecesim pertinentes."[37] Magnus seems to have taken the admonition of the emperor to report on "qualiter tu et suffraganei tui doceatis et instruatis,"[38] very seriously, so that the work of Theodulf of Orleans, several anonymous works, as well as a synodal response to the questions of the circular letter all find some voice in the relatively brief response of Magnus. This shows that at least the ecclesiastical province of Sens had a strong organizational centre, and perhaps it also shows why, since Magnus does not miss this opportunity to call upon his suffragans to discuss an eminently pastoral matter under the patronage of the emperor himself. Surely it was not lost on the

---

[37]Keefe, "An Unknown Response," p. 56, lines 1-3.

[38]Ibid., p. 88, lines 18-19.

metropolitan archbishop that the value of his answer would be increased by this action, but equally important was the discussion and correspondence this method of formulating a response would generate. Given the manuscript evidence, if this was in the mind of Magnus, he was most successful.

The library of Sens also was called upon with two portions of the response coming from Isidore's *Etymologiarum* (book 6, chapter 19, nos. 43 and 54), and two sections from *Primo paganus:* one dealing with the Chrismal veil and the other with the laying on of the hand by the bishop.

iii) Content.

The text answers the questions as follows: first is a sentence on the etymology of the term *baptism* followed material on the three immersions and the reason for the Trinitarian form. The document then answers questions of the circular letter in order with the following exceptions and additions: a) questions one and two are dealt with as a unity; b) a section on the confession of faith is added after the question on the pomps and works of the devil; c) to question 11 the touching of the ears is added to that of the nose with a mention of the *effeta* and spittle; d) the laying on of the hand by the bishop is inserted before first Eucharist and explained as the gift of the Holy Spirit; and e) the discussion on the first reception of the Eucharist is termed *communio* and not *confirmatio* as in the circular letter.

iv) Excluded documents.

Texts K16-K19 may all be eliminated from the discussion, since they are part of the collaborative process led by Magnus in the ecclesiastical province of Sens. All of these texts have passages repeated in the response of Magnus of Sens, and so are eliminated from being a direct response to the emperor. One of these, text K18, has long been considered as being from an unknown Baluze manuscript and a possible response, but R. Pokorny is able to state definitively: "Die handschriftliche Vorlage des Baluze-Druckes ist durchaus noch erhalten, der

Text selbst jedoch keineswegs ein Antwortschreiben an Karl den Großen."[39]

Texts K20 and K21 are anonymous documents which are omitted from this discussion for two reasons: First, they do not address many of the questions of the circular letter, and second they are from the province of Sens, from which there already exists the response of Magnus. Text K22 discusses only the catechetical phase of the baptismal ritual and appears, from the description by Keefe,[40] to be part of the same work as texts K20 and K21. There are no known editions of these three works.

F. Text K23: The response of Amalarius of Trier (809-814).

i) The Author: Amalarius.

Amalarius is believed to have been born near Metz in 775. He was one of the many students trained in the palace school at Aachen under Alcuin. He later became a teacher at this same school. He was metropolitan at Trier for only a few years, and for part of that time he was on a mission for the emperor, going to Constantinople in 813. Upon his return he no longer held the post of Archbishop of Trier, but is still a presence in the empire, attending several councils and issuing writings. In 835 he is appointed as administrator of Lyons, but is removed in 838, accused of not being true to the faith. He dies in Metz in 850.

ii) Sources used by the author.

Amalarius is clearly a person well versed in the scriptures and patristic sources. While this work is not in the form of a florilegium, Amalarius is still heavily reliant upon others as the base for the positions he takes. His sources fall into three categories: Scripture, liturgical books, doctors of the church.

---

[39]Pokorny, "Taufumfrage," p. 166.

[40]Keefe, "Handlist," pp. 195-196.

a) Scripture.

This is the most frequently used source (15 citations including a line by line explanation of the Lord's prayer); the Pauline letters figure most prominently. The use of the Old Testament is also frequent, although it is used allegorically (common of the time and this author in particular), to show how the Scriptures give clear commands to do what is in fact being done. For example the citation of the vision of the temple in Ezekiel 40:16 (in which Ezekiel sees angular windows) is used as a reason for the signing with the cross.

b) Liturgical books.

Amalarius makes extensive use of liturgical books in his response, especially *OR XI*. Amalarius is clear in his desire to be quite Roman, mentioning the fact that he is following the *ordo* and quoting the prayers in reference to the scrutinies, the giving of the salt, the seventh scrutiny, the touching of the ears and nose, the renunciation and the anointing.

c) Doctors of the church.

A third source is the writings of the doctors of the church. Amalarius cities extensive sections from the fathers: Augustine's *De catechizandis rudibus* in the section on the catechumenate; the letter to Boniface in the section on infant baptism; and Pope St. Gregory the Great on the meaning of anointing with oil. Amalarius either has excellent recall of specific texts on the matter or else has a fairly substantial library at his disposal, likely both. He also quotes parts of Isidore in regard to the symbol, and the letter of John the Deacon to Senarius on the exsufflation.

iii) Content.

This text does not follow the order of the circular letter. It appears that Amalarius is placing the explanations in the order in which he is normally experiences the ritual, and in fact he separates them into two halves, those of the scrutiny and those of the baptistry. While this might indicate a separate life of this document prior to 812, no evidence of this possibility is found in the manuscript tradition. Amalarius adds notes on topics not asked about by the emperor. He writes about the signing of the cross on the forehead during the scrutinies and gives an excursus on the meaning of this cross, on the reason for seven scrutinies, on genuflexions, on the Lord's prayer, as well as a summary at the end of the rites of the catechumenate before the rites of baptism. Amalarius also adds a section on the use of these rites with infants, in accord with the first question of the circular letter, but at the end of his response. Amalarius is much closer to Roman practice than any response seen so far.

The order of response is as follows, with some questions dealt with at more than one point: an extensive section on 1, 2 with catechesis, a section titled as the scrutiny (3) which deals with at length with the signing with the cross, the reasons for seven scrutinies, 9 by acolytes, genuflexion, the Lord's prayer [all of which are part of the scrutiny system of *OR XI*], 5, 9, 8, 10, the seventh scrutiny on Holy Saturday, 11 (also touching ears with the *effeta*), 14 with 6, an explanation of the meaning of the oil, 13, in this case meaning an anointing on the shoulder or arm, 14, a discussion of the meaning of the word *oil*, 6, 7, testing of the godparents, recapitulation of the catechumenate, the water rite, 16, 17, 15, 18, a long section on 1, 5, and the meaning of a suffragan. Given the fulness of Amalarius' description and his seeming interest in following the Roman ritual in all other things, it is odd that there is no mention of the final laying on of the hand or consignation by the bishop. Two explanations of this absence are possible: likely it is not mentioned because it was not present or but it could be that the rite was already a separate event not considered part of the baptismal ritual.

At the end of the response Amalarius discusses the meaning of the word *suffragan*, and prefers the meaning which would include the clergy and monastic authorities in his diocese, "aut presbiterorum, aut abbatum, aut diaconorum, aut ceterorum graduum inferiorum."[41] This does not escape the eye of the emperor who responds, first by praising the response that was sent, but then by leaving nothing unclear about the meaning of the term, "De episcopis suffraganeis ad ecclesiam Treforum in qua, Domino annuente, te praesulem esse volumus, sicut antenus nostram ordinationem et dispositionem atque iussionem expectasti...."[42] This indicates that while the emperor had gone to some lengths to re-establish the system of metropolitans and ecclesiastical provinces, it was not, at least in the mind of Amalarius, an established fact. The emperor has to exhort Amalarius to ever more dilignent ministry, including the oversight of suffragan bishops which is his responsibility.

iv) Excluded document.

Text K24 is a set of glosses on the prayers of the rite, and is from the ecclesiastical province of Trier, from which we have the response of Amalarius; thus it is excluded from this study on two grounds.

G. Text K25: The response of Leidrad of Lyons (798-814).

i) The Author: Leidrad.

Leidrad was born in Bavaria and came late to the attention of the empire. He was forty years old when he began his studies at Aachen, but once there he rose quickly, "..attaché après 782, a l'école du Palais, où it fut le disciple préféré d'Alcuin."[43] Even though he was a man of frail health, his great intellect and acknowledged holiness led him to positions of trust; the emperor sent him on two important missions to the Iberian peninsula which were both diplomatic and religious in nature. The emperor sent him there "pour mieux connâitre et y

---

[41]Hanssens, *Amalarii*, vol. 1, p. 250.

[42]Ibid., p. 251.

[43]J. Gadille, R. Fédou, H. Hours, B. de Vrégille, *Le diocèse de Lyon,* Histoire des diocèses de France, Br. Plongeron, A. Vouchez, gen. eds., new series, vol. 16 (Paris: Beauchesne, 1983), p. 51.

combattre l'hérésie adoptioniste de Félix d'Ugel."[44]

After these adventures he begged to be left in peace, but the needs of the church at Lyons led him to be appointed bishop at the age of 55 in the year 798, a position he held until 814, at which point he was allowed to retire and live out his last days in peace.

ii) Souces used by the author.

Of all of the responses examined, it is Leidrad who stands out as the great lover of the word of God. In his response to the circular letter he quotes the scriptures incessantly. Citing the creation of the world four times and Ezekiel's vision of the crystal, in which he sees a form of water, he goes on to seek out those events in scripture which involved water: the flood, the exodus, the wells dug by Abraham and Isaac, the meeting of Rebecca at a well, and so on and ending with the baptism of Christ in the Jordan, the blood and water from the side of Christ on the cross and the command after the resurrection to baptize. It is abundantly clear that the author centres the baptismal event in the midst of salvation history and, as Keefe notes:

> When Leidrad, archbishop of Lyons, began his explanation of
> baptism with the story of the creation of the world, in whose birth
> out of the watery abyss he saw the first prefiguration of the
> Christian sacrament, he captured the importance that the sacrament
> of baptism played in the Carolingian era in bringing harmony out of
> chaos.[45]

So the response of Leidrad is an epic tale of the prefiguring of Christ and baptism in the Old Testament and the full revelation of the meaning of life in Christ in the New. Unfortunately, the emperor was either not particularly interested in epics, or wanted to hear more, for after "receiving Leidrad's response,

---

[44]Ibid.

[45]Keefe, "Handlist," p. 170.

Charlemagne asked for more on the renunciation...."[46] Since Maxentius of Aquileia seems to omit this topic altogether, it may well be that the emperor wanted to hear more from this obviously gifted writer.

Leidrad uses scriptural imagery to justify the post-baptismal anointing, quotes Isidore with regard to the difference between *conpetentes* and catechumens, as well as on the symbol of the faith, and cites Augustine on several fronts: the need for the word and water to make a sacrament, the comparison between baking a loaf and making a Christian, on communion for the newly baptized. He uses Pope Gregory the Great to affirm the use of one or three immersions.

iii) Content.

Leidrad begins with a panoramic view of the meaning of baptism and its presence in the world from the beginning of time.[47] He then runs through salvation history to Jesus' injunction to baptize and from there on to his own time. He then gets down to answering the questions in the following order: 1 and 2 with catechesis, 8 and 9, 10, a discussion of the difference between catechumens and *conpetentes*, 3 with catechesis and a discussion of the *traditio symboli*, 11 (with the touching of the ears with spittle as well as indicating that other churches anoint with oil or oil and spittle and also anoint the mouth with oil), 14 and 6, 7, 4, 5. These are followed by a series of discussions on topics not asked about in the circular letter: on the etymology of the word *baptism*, the meaning of baptism, the two types of baptism (in water and in blood), how baptism requires the water and

---

[46]Ibid., p. 199, TEXT 27, note 1. See P. Jaffé, ed., *Monumenta Carolina*, Bibliotheca rerum Germanicarum, vol. 4 (Berlin: Weidmann, 1867), pp. 411-413.

[47]*PL*, vol. 99, col. 855, "Igitur rudis mundus, necdum sole rutilante, nec pallente luna, nec astris micantibus, incompositam et invisibilem materiam abyssorum magnitudine, et deformibus tenebris opprimebat. Solus *Spiritus Dei* in aurigae modum *super aquas ferebatur*, et nascentem mundum in figura baptismi parturiebat."

the word, the types of baptism in the Old and New Testaments which is used to explain the diversity in rites of his time, the water rite (whether by three immersions or by one), the validity of baptism by heretics, 16 (here he adds a discussion of the difference between this and the anointing of the forehead by the bishop), the laying on of the hand by the bishop for the gift of the Spirit, 15 (there is a reference to the turban of Joshua [Zach 3:4-5], but no explicit reference is made to a Chrismal veil), 18, 1, followed by a lengthy section on the way of life that the celebration obliges the newly baptized to follow. The description gives less emphasis to the pre-baptismal anointing than to any other part, and in fact mentions the topic only in passing, and in a simple fashion, "Unguntur etiam nunc catechumeni in pectore et inter scapulas oleo exorcizato, cum abrenuntiant Satanæ et operibus ac pompis ejus."[48] This is followed by a brief paragraph linking the act to the renunciation. To have only this out of a work of some sixteen columns in Migne seems to indicate that the meaning of these anointings was subsumed into the renunciation, even if they were still carried out. At any rate, the response covers the rest of the areas and more with an extensive work on the scriptural basis and meaning of the rites of the catechumenate and baptism.

    iv) Excluded documents.

    Text K26, an anonymous work, takes over entire sections of Leidrad, and so can be excluded from this discussion. Text K27, although it does not quote Leidrad, is evidently influenced by this response and the request of the emperor for more information on the renunciation of Satan. For although this work is based on *Primo paganus*, the section on renunciation is greatly expanded, just as Leidrad was requested to expand his thoughts on the subject. As Keefe notes, "Leidrad wrote him a long separate treatise on the renunciation of Satan and the vices (*PL*, vol. 99, cols. 873-884). This work may have had some repercussions in the

---

[48]*PL*, vol. 99, col. 858 B.

archiepiscopal province of Lyon."[49]

Text K28 quotes sections of Leidrad as does text K29, although in an
abbreviated form, and so can be eliminated from our study.

H. Text K30: The text of Jessie of Amiens (799-830).

This document is not a direct response to the emperor, since it is addressed
specifically to the priests of the diocese of Amiens. Further, the bishop, Jessie, is
a suffragan of the province of Rheims, and therefore not a recipient of the circular
letter. Still this work may be a derivative of a response to the emperor from an
ecclesiastical province which has left no other record. It may well be that Jessie
used the response of his metropolitan Vulfarius (808-816) as the basis for this
work.

i) The Author: Jessie.

Nothing is known of Jessie before he becomes bishop at Amiens in 799.
But once he comes on the scene, he is an indispensable part of the court of the
emperor. He was part of the delegation that went to Rome to settle Pope Leo's
difficulties; in 802 he went to Constantinople to help with the eventually fruitless
negotiations for the marriage of the empress Irene. He was appointed to the court
as *missus* in 805. In 809 he was traveling to Rome again, this time on a religious
mission helping to enshrine the *filioque* clause in the Nicene Creed, "fit encore
partie de la délégation chargée de faire admettre au pontife l'insertion de la
formule et sa proclamation par la chant du *Credo* comme c'était alors l'usage au
cours franque."[50]

Having been attached so closely to the emperor, the death of Charlemagne
had a profound effect on Jessie's career. He did not approve of Louis the Pious
and his administration, and supported Louis' son Pepin in his move to take over

---

[49]Keefe, "Handlist," p. 199, text 27, note 1.

[50]*Catholicisme: hier aujourd'hui demain*, s.v. Jesse, col. 729, by A. Mathon.

the throne, "Aussi n'est-on pas surpris de trouver Jessé...aux origines du complot qui, au printemps de 830 visa à remplacer Louis par son fils Pépin."[51] Jessie lost his see as a result of this action, and died six years later at the court of Lothar.

ii) Sources used by the author.

The main source for the first part of the work of Jessie is *OR XI*. Jessie essentially quotes the document for the period of the scrutinies, but interestingly changes the timing of the third scrutiny, moving the events of that liturgy to the sixth scrutiny, evidently to match the situation in his diocese. Then, after the sixth scrutiny, he goes on to explain the rest of the rites with almost no reference to this source. From this point on all is justified from scripture, with 35 different citations being made. Isidore is also cited in regard to the symbol of faith.

iii) Content.

After Jessie greets his priests and briefly states the purpose of the letter, he begins his instruction on the rites. The order of the rites is as follows: 2 (although expanded to include questioning with regard to the time for the celebration and the ministers required), the extensive section on the catechumenate taken from *OR XI* [the giving of the name, signing with the cross, the laying on of the hand, 9, and a dismissal. Then the candidates are called forward by name and there follows three sets of the following rites: genuflexion, signing with the cross, laying on of the hand, the third time this includes an exorcism (= 9), again a signing, a laying on of the hand, a genuflexion, a signing, and a dismissal. The Eucharist for the day continues with the mention of the godparents in the *Memento* of the Eucharistic prayer. This entire set of rites is repeated for the next four scrutinies, and in the sixth scrutiny on Palm Sunday, with the addition of the explanation of the symbol and the *traditio symboli*, the instruction on the four Gospels, as well as the explanation of the Lord's prayer and finally the section on the ministries involved.] This is followed by a discussion of the difference between a catechumen and a

---

[51]Ibid.

conpetens, 10, 9 (catechesis mentioned in the title, but not in the text) and 8 (catechesis is mentioned here), 11 (the touching is with saliva and includes touching the ears), 12 (in the sign of the cross), 13, 6, 7, 4, the etymology of the word baptism, water rite, 16, 17, anointing on the forehead by the bishop with Chrism and the laying on of the hand for the gift of the spirit (as 'confirmation'), a discussion on why only the bishop may do this, 18 (also 'confirmation'). The giving of salt and the exorcism are discussed at two points, at the beginning of the scrutinies as quoted from *OR XI* and a second time after the discussion of the *competente*. The dressing with the white garment is not mentioned explicitly, but the discussion on the Chrismal veil cites the image of the just standing around the throne in white robes wearing crowns.

iv) Excluded documents.

Text K31 is a set of glosses based on the prayers of the rites, and so does not match the format for a response to the emperor. Text K32 is the work of Anglimodus of Soissons (862-864/5), who was neither a metropolitan nor from the era under consideration.

I. Text K33: The response of Maxentius of Aquileia (811-833).

i) The Author: Maxentius.

An extensive search of the literature has revealed no further information concerning Maxentius. The major work of his life - some 22 years - was obviously his work as the patriarch of Aquileia, but apart from this he appears to have lived in the shadow of his famous predecessor, Paulinus.

ii) Sources used by the author.

This relatively brief response makes extensive use of the scriptures and the rites themselves. Maxentius shows us that Aquileia is truly a metropolitan place, which assimilates into its own rites whatever it judges useful. He cites *OR XI* for baptism, he uses Isidore to explain the exsufflation and he uses scripture fifteen times in making allusion and allegory with an ability unmatched in the response

72

tradition. All but one of these references are to the New Testament. He also uses
the beautiful *expositio symboli* from the *Gelasianum*.[52] Given the unsettled
situation of his diocese, it should be wondered that Maxentius responded at all, let
alone produce a work of such quality.

iii) Content.

After the greetings to the emperor Maxentius sets out his response as
follows: questions 1, 2, a description of *conpetentes*, 10, 9 and 8, 3 (including the
laying on of the hand), *signatum oleo sanctificato* (which of 12-14 is not specified,
in fact all three questions are covered since the anointing is all over the body), 6,
the entry into the baptistry and the water rite with three immersions in the Trinity,
16, 15, 17, the explanation of the symbol from the *Gelasianum* (= 4 and 5), 18.
There is almost no discussion of the renunciation of Satan, or of the pomps and
works of Satan (there is no evidence of a subsequent letter from the emperor on
this point, in contrast with that of Leidrad), nor is there a complete description of
anointing before baptism.

J. Text K34: The response of Arno of Salzburg? (785-821)

This text, although it remains unedited, has been described in detail by
Bouhot.[53] The order and content of the items discussed can be discerned from his
work. While he feels certain that this is a direct response to the emperor, there is
no protocol or eschatacol in the table he provides while editing text K36.[54] From

---

[52]See Mohlberg, Eizenhöfer, Siffrin eds., *Gelasianum*, 3rd ed., p. 50, no. 315.

[53]See Bouhot, "Alcuin et le 'De catechizandis rudibus' de saint Augustin,"
Recherches augustiniennes 15 (1980): 205-230.

[54]In the production of his edition of text K36, K34 was used as a cross-
reference. In fact it is through the work of Bouhot that the assigning of text K34
to Arno is possible; two brief references from that work make the origin of the
current text quite clear. "Vers la fin de l'été 796, Alcuin a envoyé à Arno de
Salzbourg une copie d'une lettre récemment adressée au roi, à la suite de la
soumission des Avars." (p. 199) "Un quinzaine d'années plus tard, quel autre
archevêque qu'Arno de Salzbourg pouvait insister dans sa réponse a l'enquête de

this scanty evidence it is more likely that the text is a derivative document of the response of Arno of Salzburg.

i) The Author: Arno.

Arno numbers among the many friends and disciples of Alcuin appointed as bishop. Before coming to the episcopacy he served as an abbot. After his appointment to Salzburg, Arno stands out for his awareness and energetic attention to the duties of bishop. His special concern was the quality of the clergy.

> Il ne tarda pas à se dévouer entièrement aux fonctions de sa charge, comme Charlemagne savait l'inculquer aux évêques qu'il nommait, et, par son activité et son zèle comme par sa situation dans la monarchie franque, il acquit promptement de l'ascendant sur son clergé dont ils s'occupait surtout, et un certain prestige dans les régions voisines.[55]

Arno would hold councils on a regular basis during his ministry in Salzburg, ever exhorting the clergy to fulfill their ministry. He would also retain his love for the monastic life, calling for a deeper commitment on the part of those who took religious vows in his archdiocese.

His concern for the clergy reflected an even deeper concern for the people to whom he was sent as bishop. Together with Paulinus of Aquileia he led a synod in 796 that called for an end to the forced conversions in the empire:

> They demanded an accommodation to a *gens bruta et inrationalis*, which needed instruction. Mass baptisms and force were rejected. The instruction which had to precede baptism should aim at

---

Charlemagne sur certains aspects du baptême administré aux adultes, en reprenant un texte inspiré par une lettre d'Alcuin?" (p. 200) Bouhot goes on to edit the text of K36, which is an expanded version of text K34 adding to it large passages from Augustine. In an appendix to his work he lays out the order and content of our document K34.

[55]*DHGE*, vol. 4, col. 541.

understanding and not the fear of man.[56]

The message seems to have gotten through, since the *Capitulare Saxonicum* issued in 797 accepted these principles.

Finally he was a trusted servant of the emperor, being part of the delicate mission of 799 that went to Rome to solve the legal difficulties of Pope Leo III.

ii) Sources used by the author.

This is a florilegium, citing much of Isidore (8 citations), Augustine (7 citations), three long sections from the works of Nicetas of Remensiana, *Primo Paganus* (7 citations), the venerable Bede (3 citations), Athanasius (3 citations), Jerome (2 citations), and one citation each from Gregory the Great, Leo the Great and Origen, in addition to the scriptures (11 citations).

iii) Content.

Given the outline of Bouhot, the response of Arno proceeds as follows: a discussion on making a pagan a catechumen, followed by responses to question 2 (with catechesis), 3, 6, 7, 5, 4, 8 and 9, 10, 11(with the touching of the ears), 12, 13, 14, the etymology of the word 'baptism', the water rite with three immersions in the trinity, 15, 16, 17, 18, episcopal laying on of the hand and Chrismation for the gift of the Spirit, Christian living. The focus here is on adult initiation, and so the importance of catechesis is far and away the major part of the work, both before and after the baptismal ceremonies. This is clearly a response from a mission territory, and so, given the evidence of Bouhot, there can be almost no doubt of it coming from Arno.

iv) Excluded documents.

As has already been indicated, texts K35 and K36 are either abbreviated or expanded forms of this document, and so can be set aside from the current study. Text K37, for its part is described by Keefe as being "three chapters on the

---

[56]Jedin, Dolan, Kempf, Beck, Ewig, Jungmann, gen. eds, *Handbook of Church History*, vol 3, p. 85.

catechumen, competent and creed,"[57] and so may also be set aside as not meeting the criterion of answering the questions of the circular letter.

K. Text K38: Anonymous.

This text is clearly a reworking of *Primo paganus*, and while the document lacks a protocol and eschatacol, Heer has titled it as an anonymous response to the circular letter. A more likely theory is that it is a derivative document. From the single manuscript that exists Keefe has located it in the province of Salzburg, which would eliminate it from consideration in the light of what has just gone before. However this assignment is by no means secure. In fact, the complete manuscript is listed by Keefe as originating in Northern Italy or Bavaria on the strength of the work of Bischoff. This same manuscript contains the only surviving copy of the response of Maxentius of Aquiliea, to whom this document was originally attributed.[58] The current document could equally be from Grado, for which we do not have a response. Thus, it is worthy of consideration.

i) Sources used by the author.

The main source for this document is *Primo paganus*, which is quoted in or adapted into thirteen of the nineteen sections. For example the section on the giving of the salt quotes this main source, but adds a reference to salt as a form of pablum; parts are also added on the *conpetentes* and instruction, a further reason for the touching of the nose and ears, an examination upon entering the baptistry,

---

[57]Keefe, "Handlist," p. 205.

[58]B. Pez, ed., *Thesaurus anecdotorum, nouissimus seu Veterum Monumentorum praecipue Ecclesiasticorum, ex Germanicis potissimum Bibliothecis adornata Collectio recentissima*, vol. 2/2 (Augsburg: P., M., & J. Veith, 1721-1728), col. 16., at the end of his edition adds the following note to this text: "Maxentii Epistolae mox subjuncta in eodem Codice erant quaedam dicta Colletanea de ritibus Baptismi, quae an ab eodem Maxentio ex diversis antiquorum Auctorum scriptis, an ab alio excerpta fuerint, incompertum habeo. Mihi ea ob argumenti similitudinem his haud praetermittenda visa sunt. En ergo illa."

76

additional reasons are given for the garment, the citation from the first letter of Peter on the priestly nature of the Chrismal veil is altered, there is a further reason given for first Eucharist.

ii) Content.

The order is as follows: after speaking of making a pagan a catechumen and a section on catechesis, the text answers questions 9, 10, 2, gives a section on the *conpetentes* as compared to catechumens, the giving of the name and a section on catechesis, 3, 8, the *traditio symboli*, the sign of the cross with 12, 11, 13 and 14, [6?] which is part of the admission to the font for the final testing by the presbyter including a form of a *redditio symboli*, the water rite by immersion in the name of the Trinity, 15, 16 and 17, 18, and the laying on of the hand by the bishop as a gift of the Holy Spirit. Given the great freedom with which several of the previously seen responses have dealt with the questions of the circular letter, this work is remarkably faithful to the order of the questions.

iii) Excluded documents.

Texts K39 and K40 are both found within an *interrogatio sacerdotalis*, and are far too limited to be considered as possible responses.

L. Text K41: Anonymous (Hildebald of Cologne?)

This anonymous response meets the criteria for inclusion as a response by being geographically from a province that is without a response, directed to the questions of the circular letter and in a format which is consistent with a response. The attribution to Hildebald of Cologne is made through an examination of the manuscript evidence. M. Jostes[59] at the end of the last century noted certain typical Saxon expressions, and so placed its authorship in either Mainz or Cologne; and while Jostes favored Mainz, in a more recent examination of the documents by

---

[59]M. Jostes, "Der Dichter des Heliand," *Zeitschrift für Deutsches Altertum und Deutsche Litteratur* 40 (1896): 341-368.

N. Kruse,[60] Cologne appears as the likely place of origin.

i) The Author: Hildebald.

Hildebald was a person of noble birth, and lived a life of privilege. In 791 he was appointed as archchaplain to Charlemagne. Those who held this position "were regarded as the chief advisers of the emperor, not merely in ecclesiastical, but in other, matters as well."[61] He was sent with Arno to solve the difficult situation in Rome in 799. It seems that his responsibilities to the emperor may have often found him often out of Cologne, especially after the added responsibilities of abbot of Mondsee became his in 803. He is remembered with reverence in Cologne, since to him is attributed the rebuilding of the cathedral.

ii) Sources used by the author.

This response is clearly a version of *Primo paganus,* quoting it directly in thirteen of twenty sections, however it diverges from that document largely through a greater emphasis on the meaning of the symbol, its use and transmission. This response has a distinctly liturgical flavor to it: the passage on the giving of the symbol is from the *Gelasianum,* and the *sacramentorum liber* is referred to directly in the beginning of the text. It would seem that the author is here beginning from the liturgical sources before him, the "what" of the rites, though not ignoring the questions of "why?" A special feature of the document is a single phrase in the vernacular language of the time which describes the understanding of the pomps of the devil.

---

[60]N. Kruse, *Die Kölner volksprachige Überlieferung des 9. Jahrhunderts* (Bonn: Rhemisches, 1976), pp. 89-132.

[61]H.M. Gwatkin, P. Whitney, eds., *The Cambridge Medieval History,* vol. 2: *The Rise of the Saracens and the Foundation of the Western Empire* (New York: McMillan, 1926), p. 662.

78

iii) Content.

This response alters *Primo paganus*, presumably to match local conditions, especially by moving the section on the symbol to immediately after the renunciation. There is a further accent upon the symbol, at the end of the response, in an explanation of the symbol of Nicea referring to the three hundred and eighteen fathers and an anathema upon those who do not agree. There is also the laying on of the hand by the bishop. The response is as follows: the making a pagan a catechumen, 2 and 6, 7, 3, 4, 5, 8, 9, 10, 11, 12, 13, 14, the water rite (with three immersions in the name of the Trinity), 15, 16 and 17, 18 (using the verb *confirmatur*), followed by an episcopal laying on of the hand for the gift of the Spirit and then a relatively long explanation of the symbol (= 5) and an anathema upon the Arians.

M. Text K42: Anonymous.

This text should be considered among the derivative documents. Although it is not addressed to the emperor, it does follow the general pattern of a response, and is located in the ecclesiastical province of Mainz, for which we have no known response.

i) Sources used by the author.

This text makes use of both Isidore and extensive parts of *Primo paganus*. Three of the first eight sections are adapted from both these works, and the remaining seven sections are direct quotations of *Primo paganus* with minor variants.

ii) Content.

The text covers the questions of the circular letter in the following fashion: 2, the making a pagan into a catechumen, 8, 9, 10, 4, 5, *traditio symboli*, 3, 11, a section on touching and anointing of the ears with the *effeta*, 12, 13, 14, the water rite with the triple immersion in the name of the Trinity, 15, 16 and 17, 18, followed by a section on the use of Chrism and one on the laying on of the hand by the bishop. These last two sections deserve special attention, since they provide a singular insight into the entrance of these actions into the ritual. The first of these two is described as '*nouissimum*,' and the second '*nouissime*.' In the other documents which use *Primo paganus*, the term '*nouissime*' could logically be seen as 'lastly.' In this case, however, it is impossible for both of these events to be last, and so an alternative translation would see the latter of these references as meaning 'latest' or 'newly added.' This text at least raises such a possibility, which could help to better understand the placement of what will become in a later time the sacrament of confirmation at a point which is out of place when compared with the majority of the Christian tradition, including that of Rome, from whence the ceremony arrived. This is not, however absolute proof, since the section on communion is taken from *Primo paganus* and may simply have been quoted without making any alterations.

iii) Excluded documents.

According to Keefe, text K43, like text K24, is a series of glosses on the prayers of the rite, and does not seem to address the questions of the circular letter. Texts K44, K45 and K46 all make use of *De clericorum institutione* of Rabanus Maurus[62] and so are from a later period than the focus of the current study. Texts K47 and K48 are found in the context of an *interrogatio sacerdotalis* and so are not considered, as they are not in the format of a work focused on baptism. Any relation they may have to a response would be at a tertiary level. None of the texts mentioned in this paragraph have a critical edition.

Text K49 is a very brief part of a larger work, again an *interrogatio sacerdotalis*. As it is only nine lines long in the edited text, it is surely not a response to the circular letter.

---

[62]Written in 819 according to *PL*, vol. 107, col. 203; at least after 817 according to *Rabanus Maurus: Martyologium*, ed. J. McCullogh, Corpus Christianorum Continuatio Mediaevalis, vol. 44 (Turnhout: Brepols, 1979), pp. xiv-xv.

N. Text K50: Anonymous.

This text has no protocol or eschatacol to the emperor, but its structure and content may put it among the group of the derivative documents we have seen.

i) Sources used by the author.

The main source used is the scriptures, both in quotations and in indirect references. Augustine is cited in reference to the topics of catechesis and the scrutiny, the works of the venerable Bede are referred to in reference to the touching of the ears, and the Apostles' Creed is used as the basis for the answer on the meaning of the symbol.

ii) Content.

The questions and answers follow the following topics: The giving of the name, signing with the cross, 10, catechesis and 2, 3, *traditio symboli*, 4, 5, 9, on touching the ears with saliva and speaking the *effeta*, 11 with a second mention of the ears, 8 (both ex- and insufflation), the consecration of Chrism *in caena domini* (here evidently referring to the day), 14, 12, 13, anointing the forehead with Chrism, the blessing of the water, 6 and the admission to the font, 7, the water rite which mentions immersions in the name of the Trinity, 15, 16, 17 (including why the veil is worn for seven days and taken off for the eighth), 18.

O. Text K51: Anonymous.

This document is incomplete, and in the section extant the copyist has made many errors. It lacks a protocol and eschatacol, but the first question is, allowing for the spelling mistakes, a direct quotation of the first two questions of the circular letter, and so should be considered among the derivative documents.

i) Sources used by the author.

This document is a florilegium, citing large sections of Isidore (in two separate sections) and Augustine (Tract 44 on the Gospel of John), an *expositio symboli* from an unknown source, as well as citations of an unknown sacramentary, Fulgentius of Ruspe, Eucharius of Lyons, and Placidius. The text breaks off in the midst of the section on the exorcism, while citing a passage from Zachariah.

ii) Content.

The document in its current form begins with the first two questions of the circular letter together and answers them with a passage from Isidore and the long section from Augustine. The question on the scrutiny follows, and the question on the meaning of the term *symbolum*, with seven different explanations taken from various sources. This is followed by an extensive *expositio symboli*. The origin is unknown, but it appears to be taken from an already existing source, since it ends with an exhortation, *fratres karissimi*, clearly not a term which would be addressed to the emperor. Then follow brief explanations of the renunciation, exsufflation, and exorcism. At this point the document breaks off. The first nine questions are thus answered in identical order to the circular letter.

iii) Excluded document.

Text K52 is an *interregatio presbyterorum*, and so is outside the scope of this study.

P. Text K53: Anonymous.

i) Sources used by the author.

This is a version of *Primo paganus*, which has the interesting change of the first sentence to "Et dominus Iesus primo catichuminum fecit...."[63] which introduces a description of the Gospel story of John 9:6-7 where Jesus places mud on the eyes of the blind man. The section on the symbol is expanded, however it is placed after the giving of the salt, and so is consonant with the order of the *Primo paganus* text. The sections on the pomps of the devil and the touching with spittle are also different from this main source. Another divergence from *Primo paganus*

---

[63]Dümmler, *Epistolae karolini aevi*, vol. 2, p. 535.

82

is a specifying of the Trinitarian formula in the section on the water rite.

ii) Content.

The focus on the symbol in this document is, as in the case of text K41, worthy of note. Moreover, in this text it appears that catechesis more than a liturgical rite is at the base of the explanation of the symbol. The focus upon the actual wording of the Trinitarian formula is in relation to the practice of triple immersion, which may be in response to the conflict with the church of the Iberian peninsula which had a single immersion. This may help us to tentatively place this document in the Southwest section of the empire, which is in accord with Keefe who places it in Southern France or Northern Italy.

The text has the following pattern: after the greeting the text answers questions 1, 2, a discussion of how Jesus made the first catechumen, 3, 8, 9, 10, *traditio symboli*, 4, 5, 6, 7, 11 (with the touching of the ears, both with spittle), 12, 13, 14, the water rite, as usual noting the immersions and the Trinitarian invocation, 15, 16, 17, 18, the laying on of the hand by the bishop which gives the Spirit. This is clearly in the realm of responses, but has not been assigned to any of the metropolitan archbishops.

iii) Excluded document.

Text K54 is inaccessible since it remains unedited, but as it, according to Keefe, has parts identical with text K53, it is not a response. Keefe especially notes three topics, "*opera, pompa,* and *aures.*"[64] Its French origin may yet trace it back to the influence of Leidrad and the second letter of the emperor asking for more information on two of these three topics.

---

[64]Keefe, "Handlist," p. 214.

Q. Text K55: Anonymous.

This document is likewise unedited, but the title listed by Keefe begins: "*Incipiunt questiones de rudimentis caticuminorum.*"[65] This indicates that it is not a direct response to the circular letter. Still, given the format of questions and responses as well as the similarity to text K09, this document should be placed among the derivative texts.

i) Sources used by the author.

This document makes extensive use of *Primo paganus*, citing it directly thirteen times, but amends it considerably, usually adding a definition to the beginning of each section. Of special note are the questions on the exorcism and the laying on of the hand of the bishop, the first of which adds a Trinitarian formula to the exorcism and the second of which is a new creation, the only place in the response tradition where the giving of the Holy Spirit is associated with the ascension of Jesus.

ii) Content.

The document begins with a question on why one is called a catechumen and the language it comes from, followed by a question on the Latin translation of the word. Appended to the answer to this question is the beginning of *Primo paganus*. Then come the questions on the exsufflation, exorcism which seems to include the renunciaton followed by the giving of salt. Then comes a question on why the symbol is handed on, and then on what the word *symbol* means. After this comes the question on the scrutinies, the touching of the ears and nostrils, the anointing of the chest and back with oil in the sign of the cross by a priest, followed by the question on why both chest and back are anointed. Then follow the questions on the water rite and the post-baptismal rites of the white garment, the anointing with Chrism, the veil, first Eucharist and the laying on of the hand of the bishop which is to give the Holy Spirit, the last of which is attributed directly

---

[65]Ibid., p. 215.

to the command of the Lord. Thus the questions are answered in this order: 2, making a pagan into a catechumen, 8, 9 with 6 & 7, 10, *traditio symboli*, 4, 3, 11 with the touching of the ears, 12, 13 (both anointings are done in the sign of the cross), 14, the water rite in the name of the Trinity, 15, 16 and 17, 18 and the giving of the Holy Spirit by the bishop with no specification as to how this is accomplished.

iii) Excluded documents.

Text K56 can be easily excluded on geographic and temporal grounds. It is from outside of the Carolingian empire, that is from Spain, and the author, Beatus of Liébana (ca 730 - 798), died before the circular letter was sent. Text K57 focuses only on the water rite and so addresses one of the few questions not in the circular letter, and is thus excluded.

Text K58 is clearly not a response, since it contains part of texts K33 and K30. Text K59 has similarities with text K27, and is thus also excluded.

Text K60 is more of a definition than a description, and so does not fall within the realm of possible responses. Finally, text K61 describes the ten modes of baptism from the scriptures, which places it in an entirely different literary *genre*.

5. Summary.

And so, from the documents listed by Keefe, the current study has found seven documents (texts K-01, 15, 23, 25, 33, 41 and 53) which are responses to the circular letter of the emperor and an additional ten which are derivative documents (texts K-05, 10, 12, 30, 34, 38, 42, 50, 51 and 55) for which the parent is no longer extant. Forty-three of the documents are certainly not part of the response tradition, which, with the circular letter itself (text K14), adds to the total number of sixty-one known documents on baptism from the Carolingian era. If all of the derivative documents represented different metropolitan provinces (by no means certain), this is still well within the maximum number of twenty-one possible respondents to the circular letter. The direct responses and derivatives have been examined to determine the order and number of questions which they address. The table on the following pages lays out, in summary fashion, the texts cited by Keefe and their relevance to the current study. The geographic titles are as listed in the work of Keefe.

This preliminary analysis complete, the study now moves into a synthetic phase, that of comparing the responses to try and develop a picture of the form which Christian initiation took at this moment and place in history.

86

TABLE 3

SUMMARY OF THE DOCUMENTS OF THE

'HANDLIST' OF KEEFE

Indented numbers not direct responses to the circular letter
Column A = direct responses, B = derivative documents
C = not responses, * = no edition known

Text Number			Document - grouped by location
A	B	C	I. North Italy/Switzerland
K01			Odilbert/anonymous
		K02	Related to K01
		K03	Related to K01 & K02
		*K04	Related to K01 & K02 & K03
	*K05		Answers the questions of circular letter but not addressed to Charlemagne - Always found with K01
		*K06	Florilegium always found with K01
		K07	Explanation on the stages of initiation
		*K08	Extract from Isidore *De eccl. off.* 2.25-26 Always found with K01
			II. Tours and Western France
		K09	Letter of Aluin *Primo paganus*
	K10		Not addressed to Charlemagne but in question/response form
		K11	Glosses on selected words of the rites
	K12		Not addressed to Charlemagne but in question/response form
		*K13	Excerpts from Isidore
			III. Aachen
K14			Letter of Charlemagne

			IV. The ecclesiastical province of Sens
K15			Magnus of Sens
		K16	Theodulf of Orléans
		*K17	5 passages also found in Magnus' response
		K18	Synodal response 4 passages in Magnus
		K19	In question/response format, but from the province of Sens: Morin thought it a response; Keefe, no
		*K20	Compilation of Isidore in question/response form
		K21	Related to K20
		*K22	Found in a single manuscript with K20 and K21
			V. The ecclesiastical province of Trier
K23			Amalarius
		*K24	Glosses on words selected from the prayers of the rite, similar to K43
			VI. The ecclesiastical province of Lyons
K25			Leidrad
		*K26	Part of an *interrogatio sacerdotalis*, all from K25
		K27	Supplemented form of K09 with an extended version of the renunciation of Satan
		K28	In letter form, addressed to Charlemagne, but the preface is from or used by Leidrad.
		*K29	Perhaps completion of K28; also uses K25 as source
			VII. The ecclesiastical province of Rheims
	K30		Jessie of Amiens - addressed to his priests
		*K31	Glosses on selected prayers of rites part of K48
		K32	Angilmodus of Soissons (862-864/5)

			VIII. The patriarchate of Aquileia
K33			Maxentius
			IX. The ecclesiastical province of Salzburg
	*K34		Anonymous/Arno of Salzburg? Based on K09
		K35	Abbreviated form of K34
		K36	Extended version of K34
		K37	Extract from Isidore *De eccl. off.* 2: 21-23.
	K38		Extended version of K09
		K39	*interrogatio sacerdotalis* using Isidore
		K40	*interrogatio sacerdotalis* using K09
			X. The ecclesiastical province of Cologne
K41			Anonymous/Hildebald of Cologne?
			XI. The ecclesiastical province of Mainz
	K42		An instruction based on Isidore and K09
		K43	Glosses on words from the rites similar to K24
		*K44	An instruction using Rabanus Maurus
		*K45	An instruction using Rabanus Maurus
		*K46	An instruction using Rabanus Maurus
		*K47	*interrogatio sacerdotalis* based on PRG of Mainz
		*K48	*interrogatio sacerdotalis* based on PRG of Mainz borrows parts of K47
			XII. Southern France or Northern Italy
		K49	*interrogatio sacerdotalis*
	K50		Based on *ordo* in 17 questions not addressed to Charlemagne

			XIII. Inspired by circular letter perhaps French
	*K51		Follows questions of cirular letter, not addressed to Charlemagne
		*K52	*interrogatio presbyterorum*
K53			Anonymous
		*K54	Version of K09 with part the same as K53
	*K55		Version of K09 not addressed to Charlemagne but in question/response form
			XIV. Spain
		K56	Beatus of Liébana
			XV. Problematic place of origin
		*K57	Uses Isidore, not addressed to Charlemagne but in question/response form
		*K58	Based on entire *ORDO* with parts of K33 and K30
		*K59	K09 with glosses
		K60	Definition of Baptism and on its Trinitarian form, from Isidore.
		K61	Instruction on the tend kinds of Baptism in the Old and New Testaments, partly from Isidore.

CHAPTER FOUR

THE BAPTISMAL RITES

The purpose of this chapter is to analyze those texts which have been discerned to be direct responses to the circular letter or derivative documents. But what do the responses show? B. Neunheuser in discussing these responses does not expect great theological tracts:

> Zwar dürfen wir hier keine tiefe Theologie erwarten; aber die
> Antworten....lassen doch erkennen, wie an Hand der
> zusammengestellten Väterzeugnisse langsam die Umrisse des
> künftigen theologischen Traktates über die Taufe sich deutlicher
> abheben, ähnlich wie bie Isidor von Sevilla und Ildefons von
> Toledo.[1]

Then what can be looked for in the circular letter and the responses? The descriptions in fact do provide a certain amount of direct theological reflection, but their most striking aspect is their diversity in how the responses to the questions are ordered. If these responses were designed to appease the emperor without giving any indication of a diversity of practice, one would expect the answers to be given in the order in which the questions were asked.

---

[1]B. Neunheuser, *Taufe und Firmung* in M. Schmaus, J. Geiselmann, A. Grillmeier, gen. eds., Handbuch der Dogmengeschichte, vol. 4: Sakramente; no. 2 (Freiburg in Briesgau: Herder, 1956), p. 79 (The text is unchanged in the 2nd ed., 1983, p. 97).

92

    1. The Question of the Ordering in the Texts: *Per ordinem*.

The phrase in the circular letter, "...deinde per ordinem omnia quae aguntur,"[2] indicates that the emperor is listing the questions in an order. While *per ordinem* could also be a request for a full explanation, the phrase is often used to refer to an *ordo*, or when dealing with written works to the *order* in which things are to be done. For example in the work of Jessie of Amiens, "...vocentur ipsi infantes ab acolytho infra ecclesiam, nominentur per ordinem."[3] The phrase indicates that the infants are to be called forward in order. A similar meaning is found in *OR XXVIIIA*: "14. Induti vero ordinantur per ordinem in circuitu, sicut scripti sunt, et confirmat eos pontifex...."[4] A third reference within the rites of baptism comes from a manuscript identified by De Rubeis, "Hujusce ritum accipe ex Forojuliensi codice: 4. Venientes autem omnes ad illum diem, sicut eis denunciatum fuisti faciunt ipsum scrutinium per ordinem, sicut superius est scriptum."[5] Outside the area of baptism there is a letter of Hincmar of Rheims, in which he describes his own ordination as bishop. A sentence from this letter shows the same sense of *per ordinem*:

> Et det a se ordinato pacem, et sic per ordinem ordinatus osculetur episcopos et ponatur sella iuxta eum qui illum ordinavit et sedeat ibi metropolitanus episcopus; alioquin si non esset metropolitanus, in ordine consecrationis suae sedere deberet.[6]

Finally at the head of the list of eighty-nine questions in "Qualiter episcopus suam

---

[2]Keefe, "An Unknown Response," p. 88, line 22.

[3]*PL*, vol. 105, col. 782.

[4]M. Andrieu, *Les ordines romani*, vol. 3, p. 423.

[5]B.M. De Rubeis, *Dissertationes duae*, p. 236.

[6]M. Andrieu, "Le sacre épiscopal d'après Hincmar de Reims," *Revue d'histoire ecclésiastique*, 58 (1962): 62. I am indebted to S. McMillan, snd, for bringing this reference from her work on episcopal ordination to my attention.

parrociam debet circuire," comes the sentence "Post haec ita per ordinem interroget."[7] There are other senses of the word,[8] but in general the meaning is quite similar. Now if the responses are not describing the rites in the order in which the circular letter asks them (and none of the complete responses follows this order exactly), and are not in most cases following the order described in *OR XI*, it seems that they must be describing the liturgy as it is celebrated in the place where it was written. Three other factors support this claim, one based on geography, another based upon what is known of the diversity of rites from other sources and finally an argument based upon the use of the document *Primo paganus*.

A. Geographic evidence.

The study of the responses has shown that of the responses of known authorship, Magnus of Sens is the most similar in ordering to the questions of the circular letter. That such a response would come from Sens, close to the centre of the empire, gives evidence which supports a liturgical interpretation of the ordering within the responses. The response thought to come from Cologne is also very similar to the circular letter in the order of the items discussed, and based upon the missionary nature of this territory at this time and the fact the archbishop Hildebald

---

[7]J.N. von Hontheim, *Prodromus Historiæ Trevirensis Diplomaticæ et Pragmaticæ in duas partes Tributus*, 2 vols. (Augsburg: I. & F. Veith, 1757), vol. 1, p. 353.

[8]The *Thesaurus Linguae Latinae editus iussu et auctoritate consilii ab academiis societatibusque diversarum nationum electi* (Leipzig: B.G. Teubneri, 1900 - 1990), vol. 9.2, col. 934 s.v. *ordinata* lists one of the senses as the ordering of sections of a book, and points to the work of Vitruvius, *De architectura libri*, book 4, preface, which states, "Cum animadvertissem, imperator, plures de architectura praecepta voluminaque commentariorum non ordinata sed incepta, uti particulas, errabundas reliquisse, dignam et utilissimam rem putavi antea disciplinae corpus ad perfectam ordinationem perducere et praescriptas in singulis voluminibus singulorum generem qualitates explicare." H. Romagnoli, ed., *Vitruvii, De architectura libri*, 2 vols., Romanorum Scriptorum Corpus Italicarum (Milan: S.A. Notari, 1933), p. 236.

was archchaplain for the emperor and may even have lived at court, such a similarity would be expected. In fact the major divergence is the moving of the renunciation of Satan to the beginning of the rite, an adaptation which would be necessary when working in pagan territories. Thus it seems that those areas with the closest ties to the imperial court have a response most similar to the circular letter.

B. Other sources.

Two of the responses come from sees which had well established non-Roman liturgical traditions: Aquileia and Milan. H. Boone Porter has shown that the response of Maxentius of Aquileia does, in fact, correspond to a version of the Aquileian liturgy, even though it has taken on Roman prayers.[9] The case of Milan is slightly more complicated, but there is sufficient evidence to assert that this response is a representation of the Milanese liturgy.[10] Thus in at least the two cases of Milan and Aquileia, the responses are answering the questions in their liturgical order.

C. The use of *Primo paganus*.

Several of the responses cite parts or all of this work. What is most interesting for our purposes is the use of the section on the scrutiny. This section refers to the renunciation of Satan as something which has already happened, "Tunc fiunt scrutinia, ut exploretur sepius, an post renuntiationem satanae sacra verba datae fidei radicitus corde defixerit."[11] In two of the documents studied (Text K34 and K53) this citation comes before the discussion of the renunciation. Both these documents part from the order of the circular letter at other points, so an adherence to the order of its questions cannot be postulated. It seems clear that

---

[9]H. B. Porter, "Maxentius of Aquileia and the North Italian Baptismal Rites," in *EL* 69(1955): 3-9.

[10]See the more extensive discussion above, pp. 52-54.

[11]Dümmler, ed., *Epistolae Karolini aevi*, vol. 2, p. 202.

the authors were using some other rational for the ordering of their response.

Thus given the evidence of the use of the words *per ordinem*, both in liturgical and other settings, the geographic and liturgical evidence together with that concerning the use of *Primo paganus*, there is a sufficent basis on which to assert that the order of the rites in the responses corresponds in large part to the order in which baptism was celebrated in the places where the responses were formulated. The same conclusion was reached by A. Nocent, "Quoi qu'il en soit, les réponses à la lettre de Charlemagne gardent l'ordre des rites selon la pratique des régions dont elles émanent. Elles peuvent nous être précieuses à ce titre."[12]

2. A Method for Analyzing the Rites.

There is great variety among the documents, with no two texts following exactly the same pattern. This gives evidence of a great diversity in baptismal practice, not over a period of time, but at a precise moment of history. There are four key characteristics of the texts which allow us to compare the rituals represented by these documents: a) the placement of the symbol of the faith; b) the placement of the discussion of the scrutiny; c) the point of commencement and presence of the *conpetentes* and d) the placement of the renunciation of Satan. These rites will be considered with regard to the apotropaic[13] rites (the touching of the nose and/or ears and the pre-baptismal anointings) and the exorcistic rites (the sufflation, exorcism and giving of salt). The symbol is chosen as the first point of

---

[12]A. Nocent, "Un fragment de sacramentaire de Sens au xe siècle: La liturgie baptismale de la province ecclésiastique de Sens dans les manuscrits du ixe au xvie siècles," in *Miscellanea liturgica in onore di sua emineza il cardinale Giacomo Lercaro, arcivescovo di Bologna, presidente del 'Consilium' per l'applicazione della constituzione sulla sacra liturgia*, vol. 2 (Rome/Paris: Desclée, 1967), p. 791.

[13]This term is taken from H.A. Kelly, *The Devil at Baptism: Ritual, Theology, and Drama* (Ithaca, N.Y. and London: Cornell University Press, 1985), pp. 170-171. He uses this term to distinguish rites which are not exorcistic, but rather which protect a person from future incursion by the evil one.

comparison since it is the most important question in the circular letter and was a major moment of the ritual, especially where the *traditio* and *redditio symboli* were used. The scrutiny is chosen because its placement gives it and the rites around it a completely different liturgical and theological understanding.

The presence or absence of remarks concerning the *conpetentes* is a very striking aspect of the repsonses for two reasons: first it is not mentioned in the circular letter, and so its presence in a response indicates that the rites could not be understood without this aspect. Second its presence generally marks non-Roman ritual, since the term is not found in Roman sources.[14] These rites will be taken up in turn and, with the aid of history and geography, an attempt will be made to establish the relationships which may exist between the rituals described by these documents.[15]

3. The Analysis.

A. The placement of the discussion of the symbol of faith.

There are three main placements for the symbol of faith. Documents K14, K51, K15, K05, K34, K41, and K50 all place the discussion of the symbol after

---

[14]E.C. Whitaker in the table of contents to *Documents of the Baptismal Liturgy*, 2nd ed. (London: SPCK, 1970), lists 2 Roman sources: the so-called Leonine sacramentary and the letter of John the Deacon, neither of which use the term *conpetentes*. In the category entitled *hybrid documents*, most of the sacramentaries [Mohlberg, Eizenhöfer, Siffrin eds., *Gelasianum* 3rd ed., (pp. 32-33, nos. 193-199; p. 36, nos. 225-228; p. 39 nos. 254-257; pp. 42-53, nos. 283-328; pp. 67-68, nos. 419-424; pp. 72-74, nos. 444-452), *OR XI*, and G.E. Warren, ed., *The Stowe Missal*, Henry Bradshaw Society, vol. 32 (London: Henry Bradshaw Society, 1915), pp. 24-36] do not mention the term. Only Lowe, *The Bobbio Missal* (pp. 54-60, nos. 174-193, pp. 71-76, nos. 228-254) does and not in the baptismal rites; it is found in the intercessory prayers of the Easter Vigil (p. 69, no. 225). This opinion is confirmed by A. Dondeyne in "La discipline," p. 757: "Peut-être faut-il expliquer ainsi l'apparition du mot *competens* à côté de *electus* (qui seul est romain), ainsi que le glissement quelque peu étonnant que nous avons remarqué."

[15]The reader may wish to consult Table 4 on pp. 102-109 in following this discussion.

that of the scrutiny and before the discussions of the exorcisms. In addition the symbol is usually found in close proximity to the renunciation, except in the case of K50 which places the renunciation much later in the response. Documents K53, K10, K42 and K55 place this same discussion between the exorcistic and apotropaic rites, usually associating it with the scrutiny. Documents K25, K01, K38, K30 and K23 all place a discussion of the creed in two places, both between the exorcistic and apotropaic rites and after the apotropaic rites. This second is an immediate preparation for the water rite in concert with the renunciation of Satan. K23 frames the discussion in terms of testing of the Godparents after the apotropaic rites to see if they know the symbol and the Lord's prayer. Document K01 is included in this group because of the question on the ability of the child to confess the faith for itself.[16] The citation in this response, that of John the Deacon, indicates that the Godparents confess the faith. K12 also may prove to join this group for it discusses the symbol after the apotropaic rites. This is, however the only point where it is discussed. K33 discusses the creed only after the baptismal rite.

B. The placement of the scrutiny.

All of the documents which discuss the symbol before the exorcistic rites also find the scrutiny before the exorcistic rites. In addition K12, K53, K30 and K23 place the scrutiny at this point. The remaining documents all place the scrutiny between the exorcistic and apotropaic rites.

C. The presence and placement of the *conpetentes*.

None of the documents which discuss the symbol before the exorcistic rites or only between the exorcistic and apotropaic rites describe the *conpetentes*. Those which place the symbol before *and* after the exorcism all describe the *conpetentes*. In addition, in these documents the description of the *conpetentes*

---

[16]"Utrum pueri per se confessionem faciant?" Wiegand, *Erzbischof Odilbert*, p. 34, no. 15.

98

always comes after the exorcistic rites. K33 also contains the *conpetentes*, but in this case it is found before the exorcistic and apotropaic rites.

D. The placement of the renunciation of Satan.

The renunciation of Satan is the most obvious anti-demonic part of the ritual. With the importance given to the devil throughout the history of the church, its placement is more than chance. Six texts place the renunciation before the exorcistic rites. These texts also have the placement of the symbol and the scrutiny before these rites. Text K34 inverts the renunciation and the discussion of the symbol. The sixth text (K41) places the renunciation as the first element of the rite. This appears to be what could be called a 'cultural adaptation,' since the document comes from the mission territory of Cologne. In this part of the empire the renunciation of Satan, that is of idol worship, would have been the most important part of the ritual outside of the water rite itself. Apart from this adaptation and additions at the end of the laying on of the hand and the explanation of the symbol, the text follows the order of the circular letter perfectly.

Those documents which discuss the *conpetentes* all place the renunciation after the apotropaic rites and, except for K33, with the discussion of the symbol. Documents K12, K50 and K23 also all place the renunciation at this point, although K50 has the symbol before the exorcistic rites. K53 is alone in placing the renunciation explicitly between the exorcistic and apotropaic rites. Document K55 identifies the renunciation with the exorcism. The remaining two documents, K10 and K42, do not explicitly mention the renunciation, but quote the phrase from *Primo paganus* concerning the scrutiny which implies that the renunciation has preceded the scrutiny.[17] Apart from the placement of this quote in place of the renunciation, these texts parallel K53.

---

[17]"Tunc fiunt scrutinia, ut exploretur sepius an post renuntiationem satanae sacra verba datae fidei radicitus corde defixerit." Dümmler, *Epistolae karolini aevi*, vol. 2, p. 202.

4. Conclusions.

Given the above data a number of models for baptism emerge. First is the model which has the scrutiny, symbol and renunciation at the beginning of the ritual. These also have no knowledge of the *conpetentes*. Six documents (K14, K51, K15, K05, K34 and K41) thus form a discrete type (herinafter type one), which more or less follow the same pattern: catechumen, scrutiny, symbol, renunciation, exorcistic rites, apotropaic rites, water rite, white garment, Chrism, veil, communion. The laying on of the hand of the bishop seems to be a new addition in this type, since it is found before communion (K15), after communion (K34 & K41), or is absent altogether (K05 & K14). It is not known if or where it is present in K51, since the response breaks off before this point in the ritual.

Texts K10, K42 and K55 place the scrutiny after the discussion of the symbol and between the discussion of the exorcistic and apotropaic rites. K10 and K42 have no mention of the renunciation, but seem to form a common type with K55 since they agree in so many other respects. Given their special placement of the quote from *Primo paganus* they could well be describing identical rituals. They thus form type two, which has the following structure: catechumen, exorcistic rites, (renunciation,) symbol, scrutiny, apotropaic rites, water rite, post-baptismal rites.

A third type consists of K25, K01 and K38. These all have the *conpetentes* and they also place the scrutiny between the *conpetentes* and the apotropaic rites. The apotropaic rites are then followed by the renunciation and the confession of faith in some form. Thus the order is: catechumen, exorcistic rites, *conpetentes*, scrutiny, apotropaic rites, renunciation, symbol, water rite, post-baptismal rites.

The fourth type unites those two responses which quote *OR XI*, namely K23 and K30. While one has the *conpetentes* and the other does not, there is otherwise an identity between them. The structure of these two rites is similar to that of type one, in that the scrutiny comes in the initial phase of the rite, however the renunciation is placed with the symbol immediately before the water rite, as seen in type three. The structure of this type is thus a distinct form. It begins with the catechumen and the scrutiny followed by the exorcistic rites, the discussion in one case of the *conpetentes* followed by a second discussion of the exorcistic rites, the apotropaic rites, the renunciation followed by the symbol, the water rite, the post-baptismal rites followed in the case of K23 by the final discussion of the symbol.

A number of documents remain which seem to fall in-between the other types. K12 falls between types one and four, for although it has the catechumen and the scrutiny before the exorcistic rites as in these types, and even though it places the discussion of the symbol and the renunciation after the apotropaic rites as in type four, there are no rites between the exorcistic and apotropaic rites as in type one. K50 places a first exorcism before the rites of the catechumen, but then begins with the scrutiny and symbol in type one style, while placing the renunciation after the apotropaic rites as in types three and four. These two seem to form a hybrid type between types one and four.

K53 is a distinct document as well. It begins in typical type four fashion, with the catechumen, scrutiny, exorcism and discussion of the symbol, but then places the renunciation before the apotropaic rites, the only document to do this. Further there is no discussion of either the renunciation or symbol after the apotropaic rites, which is the norm for types one and two. It therefore also seems to be a hybrid document.

Finally comes K33, which is a type unto itself. The placement of the *conpetentes* before the exorcistic rites is similar to Jessie, as is the placement of only the scrutiny between the apotropaic and exorcistic rites. But the text contains no reference to the laying on of the hand by the bishop and the order of the post-baptismal rites (Chrismation, white garment then the veil) is not found in any other text. This will be considered type five.

The analysis of these texts has shown a number of general complexes of rites which are ordered differently in different areas. They fall into four main types of rituals, plus the case of K33 (Aquileia) and three documents which fall between the established types. Table 4 on the following pages summarizes these results.

TABLE 4

COMPARISON OF INDIVIDUAL RESPONSES

Type one						Type two			Type three			Hybrid			Type four		Type five
K14	K51	K15	K05	K34	K41	K10	K42	K55	K25	K38	K01	K53	K50	K12	K30	K23	K33
											A						
		B									B						
											C						
		D															
		E															
									F								
1	1	1+2	1	G	G	1+2			1+2+I	G		1				1	1
2	2		2+I	2+I	2+6		2	2		I	2	2		2	2+H	2+I	2
							G	G						3			
					7							J					
3	3	3	3	3*	3*							3*				(3)	
													K		K		
													L		L	L	

K33	K23	K30	K12	K50	K53	K01	K38	K25	K55	K42	K10	K41	K34	K05	K15	K51	K14
		M		10													
		10															
		xx															
		L															
		M															
	9	N															
		9															
		L															
	N	M															
	Q	N										4	4	4	4	4	4	
											5		5	5	5	5	
	P	R	G+2								6	6	6	6	6	6	
			3								7	7	7	7	7	7	

K33	K23	K30	K12	K50	K53	K01	K38	K25	K55	K42	K10	K41	K34	K05	K15	K51	K14
				S											T		
	5			4									5				
U		V		5									4				
10	9	10	8														
9+8	8	9+1	10		8	9	9	8+9	8	8	8	8	8+9	9+8	8	8	8
		8+1		9	9	8	10	10	9+6+7	9	9	9	10	10	9	9	9
	10		9		10	10	2		10	10	10	10			10	?	10
			10			V+U	V	V									
							K										
					S		I	3+I+S	S		S						
					4				4	4	4						
					5					5	5						
										S							

K33	K23	K30	K12	K50	K53	K01	K38	K25	K55	K42	K10	K41	K34	K05	K15	K51	K14
3 + M	W				6 7	3 3 I + M	3 8 S		3*	3*	3*					?	
	11 + Y 11 + Z	11 + X 11 + Y	11 + X 11 + Y	X + Y +Z 11	11 + X + Y	4 + S X Y Z 11		Y + 11 + X + bb + aa	11 + Y 11 + Y	11 + Y + Z + aa	11	11	11 + X 11 + Y	Y + 11 11 + X + X + + Y + Z Z	11 + X + Y + Z		11
	14 + 6 dd 13 + ee		13 14 + L	8 cc 14													
12 - 14	12	12 + L	12 + L	12	12	12	L + 12		12 + L	12	12 + L	12	12	12 + 13	12	?	12

	K33	K23	K30	K12	K50	K53	K01	K38	K25	K55	K42	K10	K41	K34	K05	K15	K51	K14
								11										
			13	13	13	13	13	13+14		13+L	13	13	13	13		13	?	13
				14		14			14+6	14	14	14	14	14	14	14	?	14
					ff													
					gg													
				s														
	6	6	6	6	6+hh		6	[6]+ hh+T										
		7	7		7				7									
		ii					1											
			4						4									
									5									
				B					B					B				
									jj									
									C									
														E				
									F									
	hh								ii									

	K14	K51	K15	K05	K34	K41	K10	K42	K55	K25	K38	K01	K53	K50	K12	K30	K23	K33
																	nn	
					D	D+E	D+E	D+E	D+E	D	D+E	D+E	D+E	D+E	D+E	D+B+E	D	D+E
	15	?	15	15	15	15	15	15	15	kk	15		15	15	15			
	16	?	16	16	16	16+17	16	16	16	16+pp	16+17	16	16	16	16+17	16	16	16
																15?		15
	17	?	17		17		17	17	17			17	17	17		17	17	17
			M							M+rr		15		oo		qq+rr	15	
			rr							15 (17?)						M		
																pp		
																		4
																		5
	18	?	18	18	18	18	18	18	18	18	18	18	18	18	18	18	18	18
					M+rr+ff	M+rr	M+rr	ff+M+rr	rr		M+rr	M+rr	M+rr		M+rr			
										1							1	

K14	K51	K15	K05	K34	K41	K10	K42	K55	K25	K38	K01	K53	K50	K12	K30	K23	K33
					5						ss					5	
				uu					uu								
					tt											vv	

Key:

Numbers = questions of the circular letter (Table 2).

* = scrutiny reference from *Primo paganus*

Letters:

A=scriptural warrant for baptism
B=etymology of the word 'baptism'
C=baptism in water and the word
D=immersions
E=baptism in the Trinity
F=discussion of salvation history
G=making a pagan a catechumen
H=discussion of needed ministers
I=catechesis
J=Jesus made the first catechumen
K=the giving of the name
L=signing with the cross
M=the laying on of the hand
N=genuflexion
O=repetition of 'N, L, M' three times ending the third
  time with the exorcism (*OR XI*)
P=explanation of the Lord's prayer
Q=the reason for seven scrutinies
R=the repetition of the rites on the second to the sixth time,
  with the sixth time adding the *traditio symboli*
  and the handing on of the Gospels and the Lord's prayer
S=*traditio symboli*
T=confession of the faith
U=*competentes*
V=the difference between
  catechumens and *competentes*
W=the seventh scrutiny
X=touching with spittle

Y=touching the ears
Z=the *effeta*
aa=use of oil
bb=touching the mouth with oil
cc=the consecration of Chrism on Holy Thursday
dd=the meaning of oil
ee=anointing the shoulder or arm
ff=anointing with Chrism
gg=the blessing of the water
hh=being admitted to the font
ii=the testing of the godparents
jj= baptism and sin
kk=baptism by heretics

nn=recap of the catechumenate
oo=why the veil is worn for a week and then taken off on the eighth day
pp=anointing with Chrism by a presbyter compared to the signation of the bishop
qq=anointing by the bishop
rr=gift of the Holy Spirit from the bishop
ss=bare feet
tt=an anathema against the Arians
uu=Christian living
vv=the meaning of suffragan
xx=dismissal

PART THREE

SYNTHESIS

INTRODUCTION

Thus far the sources have been subjected to a scientific analysis simply on a basis of what the texts say. At this point begins the process of synthesizing the rituals which the sources describe. In chapter five the sources for each type will be taken as a unit to develop liturgical models for these types, and then in chapter six these models will be set in theological comparison to each other in order to seek the similarities and divergences of the ritual of baptism in the empire in the year 811/812.

CHAPTER FIVE

LITURGICAL SYNTHESIS OF THE TYPES

1. Type One.

This type is represented most clearly by six documents: the circular letter
(K14), the partial anonymous response (K51), the response of Magnus of Sens
(K15), an anonymous document from Northern Italy or Southern Switzerland
(K05), an anonymous document, likely a derivative of the response of Arno of
Salzburg (K34), and an anonymous response almost certainly derived from the
response of Hildebald of Cologne (K41). The general structure of the rite follows
the order of the circular letter.

A. The making of a catechumen (Q01 & Q02).[1]

The ritual begins with the making of the catechumen. Generally the rites
seem to be focused on the need for catechesis. In places on the edge of the
empire, such as Salzburg and Cologne, there was a greater emphasis on the
catechizing of pagans coming over to the faith. But even in the centre of the
empire there was still a remnant of the catechetical nature of the entry into the
catechumenate. In Sens the rite is not specified, but it might be seen as the start of
a period of hearing and learning, "ut audiat et discat antequam ad sacrum accedat
fontem...."[2] This may well be a part of the ritual, since many of the candidates are
infants and, "tamen per corda et ora tenentium eos fides confitetur catholica...."[3]

---

[1]References to the question numbers from Table 2 on p. 51 will be given with
the signal 'Q', thus Q01, Q02 and so on.

[2]Keefe, "An Unknown Response," p. 57, lines 26-27.

[3]Ibid., p. 58, lines 40-41.

The circular letter itself gives no further clues, except that even if the candidates are children they are still made catechumens, "cur primo infans catechuminus efficitur."[4]

In the response from Cologne, this making of a catechumen has been affected by the need to renounce pagan worship, and so the renunciation of the devil is used as the rite for the making of a catechumen. Even so the purpose of the catechumenate still seems bound up with the teaching of the faith.

The anonymous text K05 uses Isidore and *Primo paganus* to indicate that the entry into the catechumenate is a matter of learning the precepts of the law. Text K34 likewise stresses the importance of education in the rites of the catechumenate.

B. The scrutiny (Q03).

If the emperor was aware of a Roman system of scrutinies he does not show it at this point, since he asks about the scrutiny in the singular. The response of Magnus, the anonymous texts K05, K34 and K51 also place the scrutiny in the singular. The Cologne ritual is again diverse in that there are more than one, and they are taken from the *sacramentorum liber.*[5] The ritual of Cologne seems to have used this book, but only insofar as it served them. The placement of the renunciation at the beginning of the ritual and the tying of scrutinies (in the plural) to this rite shows a typical form of liturgical development, that of holding to the known format, but adding in and adapting as necessary to the needs of the time.

Apart from this innovation, however, all the rituals have the scrutiny as the first rite after making a person a catechumen. This gives a specific understanding of the process of making a Christian and changes the meaning of the catechumenate. In these cases the scrutiny is not a catechetical tool to see if the faith has been learned. Its placement at the start of the ritual before the discussion

---

[4]Ibid., p. 88, lines 20-21.

[5]See Hanssens, "Deux documents," p. 79, line 18.

of the symbol means that the scrutiny is rather a test to see if the catechumens have in fact given up idol worship as a result of their initial catechesis and so are now ready to learn the symbol of faith..

C. The symbol of faith (Q04 & Q05) and the renunciation (Q06 & Q07).

At this point five of the rituals (K34 excepted) agree on the discussion of the symbol of faith. The circular letter devotes two questions to this area, and from the length of question five it is clear that this was a central point in this inquiry. While the formula in the circular letter could be from either the Apostles' or what has become known as the Nicene creed, the formula from Cologne (K41) and the partial document (K51) is clearly the Apostles' creed. This is reinforced by the fact that the writer of K51 is clearly aware that the version of the symbol of the Nicene fathers has become a true mark of orthodoxy against Arianism and so adds it[6] on to the end of his response together with an anathema against Arian Christology. The response from Sens has a somewhat different symbol. Text K05 and K34 do not quote the symbol at any length, and so which form it takes cannot be discerned.

The response from Cologne shows that a question/response format is being used at this time, but clearly not associated with the immersions. The rubrical indication that the godfather is to respond indicates the presence of this ministry as well as the fact that we are dealing, even in this mission territory, with a large number of infant candidates. In Sens we know that there was some form of oral response by those holding the infant candidates, but the text still implies the possibility of a response from adult candidates.[7]

---

[6]The creed of the 318 fathers (without the additions attributed to the first council of Constantinople), which ended with the brief statement of belief in the Holy Spirit; see Hanssens, "Deux documents," p. 80, lines 20-29.

[7]Keefe, "An Unknown Response," p. 58, line 40, "quamvis parvuli per se profiteri non possint," the word *quamvis* indicating at least the possibility that this was an exceptional method, and that there were still some who could respond for

The placement of the symbol before the renunciation is quite novel, since the form in the Roman rituals have the renunciation of Satan before the profession of faith.[8] This Roman form is found in K34, although it remains part of type one, since in all other aspects if follows this form exactly. This gives a very different understanding of the role of the symbol, indicating that in order to be able to renounce the power of Satan one must first have the armor of the symbol.[9]

The evidence seems to clearly bind the renunciation with the giving of the symbol. In Sens it is placed between the giving of the symbol and what appears to be the remnants of a *redditio symboli*, "Quam abrenuntiationem recte confessio sanctae trinitatis sequitur...."[10] At any rate what is clear is that the renunciation and confession of the symbol of faith are seen as two parts of the same act. There is only passing reference to what the pomps and works of Satan are in the responses of this type. Keefe points to the phrase the response from Cologne has at this point, where 'his pomps and his works' are found in Old High German, "siniu gelpanda pardo sinen willen."[11]

In all of these rites the giving of the symbol appears to be associated with becoming a catechumen. In none of the cases is it found associated with the water rite.

---

themselves.

[8]See the discussion on this in the following chapter, p. ???

[9]See Bouhot, "Alcuin," p. 222: "Instructus igitur et enutritus ad fidem Christi, catecuminus iam ad exocizandum ducatur, et diabolo repudium dicat et dignum se diuinae gratiae praeparet."

[10]Keefe, "An Unknown Response, p. 58, lines 59-60.

[11]Hanssens, "Deux documents," p. 79, line 16. This phrase has taken up the interest of those studying the origins of the Germanic languages. See N. Kruse, *Die Kölner volksprachige*, pp. 89-132. On pp. 108-122 the words are divided and translated as follows: siniu= his, gelp = pomps, ardo = and, sinen = his, uuillen = works.

D. The exorcistic rites (Q8-Q10).

These rites, the breathing upon the candidate (Q08), the exorcism itself (Q09) and the giving of salt (Q10) all have as their goal the removal of the remnants of the influence of Satan from the candidate. These rites show the need to have Satan expelled, since the renunciation by the person is not seen as sufficient to expel the prince of darkness. The first act is the breathing upon the candidate. The term *exsufflantur* is used in the partial response (K51), the Cologne response (K41), K05, and the response from Salzburg (K34), *insufflantur* in the circular letter (K14) and Magnus (K15). If Bragança is correct this indicates that K05 and K51 should come from the area of Cologne and Salzburg.

This rite is followed by the exorcism proper, which is seen as putting the devil to flight. At this point K51 ends, before any comment on the last of the exorcistic rites and any hint of what follows. Given the agreement of this text with the others of type one to this point, the likely conclusion is that the lost portion of this document would continue to follow this type.

Finally comes the giving of salt, which has two different senses in this ritual type. In the response from Cologne its purpose is to remove from a person that which is rotten because of sin, while in Magnus and K05, the sense is one of partaking of the salt of wisdom. The response from Salzburg understands the rite in both of these senses. This shows that in the centre of the empire there was a lesser emphasis on Satanic possession, and so new meanings were evolving to suit the setting. The rite is still placed with the other two exorcistic rites, showing the conservation of the original meaning of this set of rites, even if for Magnus and K05 it is already become an apotropaic rite.

E. The apotropaic rites (Q11-Q14).

These rites included the touching of the nose (Q11) and at times the ears and even the mouth of the person, and two prebaptismal anointings (Q12 - Q14). Magnus and K34 reveal a more developed rite of the *effeta*, as well as the use of spittle and the touching of the ears, none of which is mentioned in the circular letter or the response from Cologne. Magnus,[12] while mentioning the devil in the anointings and touching rites, indicates that the current rites are to preserve the person from future error, leaving Satan out of the picture. K05 falls between Sens and Cologne, having the *effeta* but not the touching of the ears or mention of saliva.

The sense of these rites as apotropaic, as a form of preventative medicine is clear in Magnus, who makes a wonderful reference to every breath a person draws as being in the service of Christ.[13] The touching of the ears is for the hearing of the message of Christ and the rejection of the message of Satan.

The two anointings are asked about individually in the circular letter, an anointing of the chest (Q12), and of the back (Q13) and then a question on why both the chest and back are anointed (Q14). The response from Cologne speaks of an anointing of the chest with the sign of the cross, a signing of the back and then gives an explanation why, "Item in pectoris et scapule unctione...."[14] indicating an explanation of why there are two anointings. The response uses almost the identical wording of *Primo paganus*. The response from Sens uses essentially the same language. Text K05 describes the anointing in terms of a further purification of those things which are symbolized by the chest and back, that is to protect the newly cleansed seats of thoughts (heart) and action (back) from further incursions by the evil one.[15] Text K34, like Magnus makes a quotation from *Primo paganus*

---

[12]See Keefe, "An Unknown Response," p. 59, lines 74-85, which includes verbs such as *permanserit* and *perduret*.

[13]Keefe, "An Unknown response, " p. 59, lines 75-77: "...nares tanguntur ut quamdiu vita comes et flatus vitae in naribus et olfactus permanserit, assidue in Christi servitio perduret...."

[14]Hanssens, "Deux documents," p. 80, line 2.

[15]Keefe's unpublished edition of K05, lines 14-15 reads: "et propterea unguitur pectus et scapulae ut mens purificetur et actio, quae significatur per pectus et scapulas."

on this matter.

The sense of these rites is clearly a preservation from future incursions of evil. The person is free from Satan, having just completed the renunciation and exorcistic rites. In all the documents dealt with the apotropaic rites follow the exorcistic, thus giving further weight to the argument that they are not in themselves exorcistic, but rather a sealing of the new person, the guarantee that they will not be again possessed by evil as they approach the font of life.

F. The water rite.

The central rite, the water bath, is little mentioned in these responses with the exception of the response from Salzburg. In this document (K34) there is an exceptional florilegium on the water rite. This quotes Isidore, the Canticle of Canticles, Augustine three times, Athanasius twice, the Gospels twice, Pope St. Leo the Great and *Primo paganus* each once. This extensive section on the water rite discusses the meaning of the water rite and the invocation of the Trinity, its parallel in the death, burial and resurrection of Jesus, and the role of the Spirit in the rite.

For his part Magnus makes only passing reference to the water rite, "Post sacrae regenerationis lavacrum...."[16] while the circular letter makes no reference to it at all. The Cologne response gives us details of the rite: "Et sic in nomine sancte trinitatis trina submersione baptizatur, id est in nomine patris et filii et spiritus sancti."[17] Three details of the rite emerge from this sentence: i) baptism is in the name of the Trinity; ii) baptism is by immersion and iii) there are three immersions. The formula is Trinitarian, but could be in either the active or passive voice. The triple immersion makes it clear that the single immersion which had been part of the dispute concerning the adoptionist heresy in the Iberian peninsula is not foreseen in this ritual. The method of baptism is still by immersion.

---

[16]Keefe, "An Unknown Response," p. 59, lines 85-86.

[17]Hanssens, "Deux documents," p. 80, lines 3-5.

In all of these rituals the symbol does not seem to be associated with the entry to the font.

G. The post-baptismal rites (Q15-Q17).

These explanatory rites, the robing with the white garment (Q15), the anointing with Chrism (Q16) and the placing of the Chrismal veil (Q17) follow the same order in all five complete examples of this type. The sense of these rites is the royal and priestly role of the newly baptized. The prophetic aspect is absent, not only in this type, but throughout all the sources taken up in this study.[18]

The laying on of the hand by the bishop is found in three of the complete responses even if it is absent in the circular letter. The responses from Cologne and Salzburg place it at the very end, after communion, which may reflect the practice of wearing the white robes for seven days, at the end of which would be the laying on of the hand. Magnus seems to agree with the emperor that it is not part of the ritual of baptism at all: "Peractis autem omnibus baptismatis sacramentis, novissime per manus impositionem a summo sacerdote...."[19] The term *peractis* indicates this separation, and so *novissime* which can mean either 'last of all' or 'the newest thing' could here be taken to have this second sense. This interpretation is supported by the variety of the placement of this rite, which shows it does not have a firmly established place in the ritual. Its absence from K05 may indicate that there were places in which this rite was not practiced.

There are signs here of the fully developed sacrament of confirmation of succeeding centuries. The sense is that of the gift of the Spirit at the hand of the

---

[18]This absence is surely worthy of further study; still a possibility comes to mind for this absence: It could be because of the absence of anything which resembled a prophetic ministry in the society. Priests and Kings were known and understood in this time, prophets were not. A similar difficulty is seen in our time with relation to kingship, especially in societies where republican democracy is considered the only just way to run a society.

[19]Keefe, "An Unknown Response," p. 60, lines 98-100.

bishop. Text K05 explicitly mentions the use of Chrism and separates the giving of the Spirit from the water rite, claiming that the water rite is only for the forgiveness of sins. The giving of the Spirit in text K34 is seen in the laying on of the hand of the bishop.

H. First Eucharist (Q18).

The celebration of the baptismal Eucharist is presumed in both the circular letter and all the responses studied as being the completion of baptism. In the response of Magnus there are indications that this presumption is being challenged. Not only does the laying on of the hand by the bishop intervene before the strengthening by the body and blood of the Lord, but Magnus goes to some lengths to defend the practice of first Eucharist as part of the celebration of initiation: "Morum istum accipiendae eucharistae a domino traditum ecclesia tenet...."[20] It seems that already there are those who would not see the reception of the Eucharist as the natural conclusion of the baptismal act, who would call for the separating of the Eucharist from the rest of the ritual, and so the Lord himself is invoked as the originator of the rite.

I. Conclusion: the ritual of Aachen and the centre of the empire.

The documents of type one have revealed a consistent ritual, with a structure which can be compared against the other types. The following summary lists the main elements of the ritual in sections. The table at the end of this chapter compares the different rituals.[21]

---

[20]Ibid, lines 113-114.

[21]See Table 10 on p. 150.

Table 5

Ritual of Type One

1. Making a Catechumen	
2. The Catechumenate	Time of instruction in the law and the symbol of faith Scrutiny (perhaps only one originally, more under Roman influence) Giving of the symbol (probably the Apostles' creed), in some places given in a question and answer format Renunciation of Satan Exorcistic rites (exsufflation, exorcism, salt) Apotropaic rites (touching of nose and other parts, anointings of the chest and back)
3) The Water Rite	
4) The Explanatory Rites	White garment Anointing with Chrism Veiling
5) Communion	
6) Laying on of the hand	Not in all responses and found at various places when present - a later addition

The ritual as described has shown the placement of the symbol with the renunciation before the rest of the rites, with the exorcistic rites followed immediately by the apotropaic ones, which in turn lead directly to the font. The post-baptismal rites and first Eucharist follow, with the laying on of the hand seemingly added on wherever it was convenient. There are indications in the responses of the ministry of the Godparent in addition to that of the bishop and presbyter. Finally there is an indication of a time of catechesis in the rite from

123

Cologne, but this may be only a reference to the giving of the symbol, and so the ritual may already be taking place in the course of a single celebration.

2. Type Two.

Type two liturgies include three anonymous documents: K10, K42 and the unpublished K55. All three follow essentially the same pattern.

A. The catechumenate and the exorcistic rites (Q01 & Q08-Q10).

The discussion of the catechumenate is followed immediately by the exorcistic rites in all three examples of this type, giving the entry into the catechumenate the flavor of a battle with Satan. The sense is that the beginning of the catechumenate is accomplished by the exorcistic rites. As a result, the whole ritual is more somber. To become a Christian is as much a question of chasing the devil away as a coming to belief in the Trinity. The anti-demonic nature of this first element of the rituals is shown even more clearly by the placement of the renunciation of Satan at this point in text K55.

B. The symbol and the scrutiny (Q04-Q05 & Q03).

All three documents briefly discuss the symbol of faith. None of them give an actual text of the symbol, but texts K10 and K42 outline the basic Trinitarian faith. The symbol appears to form a major part if not all of the catechesis, since it is precisely on the symbol that the scrutiny is focused. All three cite the phrase from *Primo paganus* which describes the scrutiny as a test to see if the faith has been learned once the renunciation has been completed. The exorcistic rites evidently suffice as the renunciation in texts K10 and K42. At any rate the point is that the phase (of indeterminate length) of the catechumenate has become a time of specific learning with an exam testing one's knowledge at the end, the scrutiny.

C. The apotropaic rites (Q11-Q14).

With such a stress on the combat with the devil, what then happens to the apotropaic rites? Surprisingly they retain most of their normal meaning, although in some places the ongoing fight against Satan is evident. Texts K10 and K55 make use of *Primo paganus* to indicate that the rites of the touching of the nose and ears are for endurance in the faith, while the anointings are to act as a shield against the devil and an inspiration to do good works. Text K42, however, does not make full use of this source. Instead, while the touching of the nose is as in the other two documents, the touching of the ears is to allow Christ and the spirit of wisdom to enter, and to allow the catechumen to enter into the wisdom of faith.[22] The anointings are explained in the same fashion as in texts K10 and K55.

    D. The water rite and post-baptismal rites (Q15-Q18).

    In all three cases the anointing leads immediately to the font. In these rites, as in type one, the symbol is not associated with the water rite.

    From this point until the laying on of the hand of the bishop all three documents are essentially quotations of *Primo paganus*, so their similarity of concepts will not be a surprise. The vesting is followed by the anointing and the veil and then first reception of the Eucharist.

    K55 breaks from the other two in the discussion of the laying on of the hand of the bishop in order to attribute the action to the authority of Christ himself, citing the Johannine Easter text (John 20:23) as the basis for the gift of the Spirit. This amendment to the source text indicates that still at this time the act was in question, needing the authority of Christ himself to justify it.

    E. Conclusion: The ritual of three anonymous documents.

    The ritual described by this type is similar to type one, but has several distinctive features. Items worthy of note include that the symbol of faith is not associated with the water rite, and that the exorcism is at the beginning of the rite, so the demonic aspects seem to be in higher profile.

---

[22]"Scriptum est in evangelio effeta hebraice latine quod est adaperire. Id est ut per aurem aperiatur ingressus in homine xristo domino nostro et ille implebit eum spiritu sapientiae et intellectus, et reliqua. Et item: tanguntur sanctificationis oleo aures eorum quia per eas ad intellectum fides ingreditur, et reliqua." De Clerq, C., "Ordines unctionis infirmi IXe et Xe siècle." *EL* 44 (1930): 121, lines 28-31.

Table 6

Ritual of Type Two

1) Making a Catechumen	(Renunciation) Exorcistic rites (exsufflation, exorcism, salt)

2) The Catechumenate	Giving of the symbol
	Scrutiny based on the symbol
	Apotropaic rites (touching of nose and
	    ears, anointings of the chest and
	    back)

3) The Water Rite	
4) The Explanatory Rites	Vesting Anointing with Chrism Veiling
5) Communion	
6) Laying on of the hand	

3. Type Three.

The Type three liturgies, represented by K25 (Leidrad of Lyons), K38 (Anonymous) and K01 (Odilbert of Milan), are distinguished by the presence of the exorcistic rites before any reference to a scrutiny (as in type two), the clearer distinction between *conpetentes* and catechumens, the placement of the renunciation after the apotropaic rites and the placement of the discussion of the symbol between the exorcistic and apotropaic rites (also as in type two). The fact that the response of Odilbert is not a completely separate type speaks more to the ongoing variety of rituals in Gaul than to any Romanization on the part of Odilbert or the church in Milan.

A. Preliminaries.

All three of these documents begin by placing baptism in the larger setting. In K38 the reference is pastoral, to the training of a catechumen in the faith and the cult of the living God, using a citation from Isidore,[23] while in the case of Leidrad and Odilbert the setting is scriptural.

B. The catechumenate and exorcistic rites (Q02 & Q08-Q10).

The type three liturgies demonstrate a developed understanding of the place of the catechumenate (Q02). In both Leidrad and the anonymous document there is an explicit reference to a time of catechesis, while in Odilbert the reference to catechumens as 'hearers' would point in the same direction. There is no indication of the duration of this time.

In all three cases, however, the catechumenate seems to begin with the exorcistic rites of the exorcism proper (Q09), exsufflation (Q08) and giving of salt (Q10). Odilbert and Leidrad also refer to an anointing at this point.[24] Just what the anointing is to signify is not clear, and, in at least the case of Odilbert, the passing nature of the mention may be an accident of the sources being used. Still its presence is worthy of note. In Leidrad,[25] there is no doubt that it is Satan who is being directly attacked in this rite. The exorcism of those to be baptized is compared to that of the *energumini*,[26] and the scriptural reference is to the demon

---

[23]See Heer, *Ein karolingischer Missions-Katechismus: Ratio de cathecizandis rudibus und die Tauf-Katechesen des Maxentius von Aquileia und eines Anonymus in Kodex Emmeram. XXXIII saec. IX*, Biblische und Patristische Forschungen, vol. 1. Freiburg im Breisgau: Herder, 1911, p. 97. "Hic a sacerdote instruitur, quomodo credere debeat, et exortationis praeceptum accipit, qualem se ad fidei regulam et ad cultum dei uiui debeat exhibere."

[24]See *PL*, vol. 99, col. 856: "Exorcizantur primum, deinde salem accipiunt et unguntur."

[25]*PL*, vol. 99, cols. 856-857.

[26]Ibid., col. 856, "Exorcismus...contra immundum spiritum pro energumenis sive catechumenis factus...."

in the man possessed that Jesus rebukes. This seems to indicate a strong relationship between the exorcism used at baptism and that used in cases of demonic possession. The giving of the salt is clearly not on the same level in the mind of Leidrad, since he attributes it not to Jesus but to the Fathers,[27] and uses the image of Lot's wife (Gen 19:26) who looked back against God's command, as well as the use of salt in pledges to explain its meaning. Those renouncing Satan by the salt of wisdom will never turn back. This rite has the flavor of an apotropaic rite, but it is clearly a part of the exorcism, being the seal or pledge of that act.

C. *Conpetentes.*

All three documents make a clear reference to the difference between catechumens and *conpetentes* at this point in the ritual. In Leidrad, however, this difference is somewhat unclear as he continues to refer to the candidates as catechumens after this point. Still Leidrad fits the pattern of the bipartite structure, since at this point comes the reference to the scrutiny (in the singular, as in the type one liturgies).

It is also at this point, the entry to the *conpetentes*, that there is the *traditio symboli*, and the beginning of another period of presumably more intense catechesis. The goal of the catechesis is clear: to learn the symbol and pure faith. As part of this process the scrutinies (Q03) are celebrated. Although the number is not specified, the goal is to test the faith and to prepare to renounce the devil, which is the climax of this phase of the ritual and the moment of entry into the baptismal rite itself.

D. Apotropaic rites (Q11-Q14).

Between the exorcistic rites and the renunciation are the apotropaic rites. They seem to have become somewhat lost as an entity in this type of ritual, and their meaning varies widely.

---

[27]Ibid., "...a Patribus ideo est institutus...."

i) The touching of the nose (Q11) (and ears).

The touching rites in both Leidrad and Odilbert involve the use of spittle and all three include a touching of the ears as well as the nose. Here the purpose remains clearly apotropaic; the nose is touched so that henceforth the action of breathing, so tied up with the life of a person, may also be linked with the works of faith. The touching of the mouth is also mentioned as an extant practice by Leidrad, but he says it is done by other churches, not his own.

ii) The anointing of the chest and back (Q12 - Q14).

These rites seem to have undergone an adaptation in the ritual of Lyons, since they are tied to the renunciation. This may be due to the fact that the infants, who must surely have been the major part of the candidates in this city, could not respond for themselves, so such corporeal rites with 'exorcized oil' would reinforce the renunciation on the part of the godparent. Alternatively this could be evidence of a Roman influence, since the *Gelasianum* has this ordering of the anointing.[28] The rites are seen as a clearing out of the devil. The renunciation is tied specifically to these anointings because, as Leidrad tells us, "...cor hominis est sedes erroris et vitiorum cum a diabolo possidetur...."[29] This physical location of Satan in the heart of the person may be what leads to a difference in the meaning of the rites of anointing from the an apotropaic form to this exorcistic version. In the other two documents the meaning is apotropaic, for Odilbert as protection from future incursion by Satan, and in the anonymous response as perseverence in faith and good works.

---

[28]See Mohlberg, Eizenhöfer, Siffrin, eds., 3rd ed., no. 421, p. 68.

[29]*PL*, vol. 99, col. 858.

E. Renunciation (Q06) and adherence (Q04 & Q05).

At this point in all three rites comes the final test, which leads directly to the water rite itself. Leidrad is absolutely clear that at this point the symbol plays a prominent part. The *redditio symboli* may not be a functional reality for the candidates, but the questioning as to the content of the symbol is still a part of the ritual. The anonymous document likewise calls on the presbyter to test the candidates before admitting them to the font. In Odilbert this aspect of giving back the faith is also present, since this is the point his source chooses to discuss the question of children who cannot respond for themselves.

F. The water rite.

Following from this return of the faith is the water rite itself. All three documents mention the image of the Trinity whose name is invoked in baptism, but each has other specific accents. Leidrad focuses more on the scriptural imagery, including the Red Sea crossing, as well as the two types of baptism, in water and in blood, and the two ways of baptizing, with one immersion or three. The reference to single immersion testifies to its continued existence, although not in the church at Lyons. Leidrad mentions, as does Odilbert, the image of the entombment of Christ. The anonymous document, citing *Primo paganus*, speaks of the three steps of sin which lead to death as part of the baptismal symbolism.

From these documents six things can be deduced: i) baptism is in the name of the Trinity; ii) the anonymous document, by indicating that baptism occurs "...per inuocationem iterum sanctae trinitatis...."[30] indicates that the question and answer format is likely not in use; iii) baptism is by immersion in all three sources; iv) in these three sees there are three immersions; v) Leidrad indicates that there still exist those who baptize by a single immersion; and vi) from the anonymous document there is at least a hint that the font for baptism has three steps from the reference to the third step or level of sin. This last assertion is not absolutely

---

[30]Heer, *Ein karolingischer Missions-Katechismus*, p. 100.

certain, since the reference is using another source or could alternately be attesting to a triple immersion.

G. The post-baptismal rites (Q15 - Q18).

Of the three rituals described in these responses, only the anonymous document places the clothing with the white garment first, as it is found in the circular letter (Q15). In both Milan and Lyons, perhaps reflecting a warmer climate, the anointings maintain their full vigor. There is a mention of the garment coming before the anointing in Odilbert, but this is because the florilegium which Odilbert uses cites a source which places the garment first; the chapter on the garment will not come until after the covering by the veil. The head is anointed with Chrism by a presbyter.

In Leidrad the anointing is completed by the sealing of the bishop and then the vesting, in which may have included the veil. It would seem an eminently practical way of proceeding, an anointing with Chrism, the blessing by the sign of the cross on the forehead by the bishop, perhaps using the Chrism which was already flowing down from the head of the person, and then the vesting with both the veil (if the scriptural references to the turban of the high priest actually refer to the veil) and the white garment. This would then lead to first Eucharist, a practice which for both Leidrad and Odilbert seems to be under some attack. For Odilbert and K38 the laying of the hand of the bishop follows first Eucharist. Odilbert also adds a section on the need for bare feet, taken from the letter of John the Deacon, a Roman source. Leidrad completes his work with discussion of questions concerning the baptism of infants and heretics, and finally the consequences of baptism in life.

H. Conclusion.

The ritual of type three takes on a distinctive shape and has two special features: the ongoing presence of the *conpetentes* and a strong emphasis on catechesis.

Table 7

Ritual of Type Three

1) Making a catechumen	An important time of instruction
2) The Catechumenate	Exorcistic rites (exorcism, exsufflation, salt) In some cases an anointing
3) The *Conpetentes*	Giving the symbol Catechesis and scrutinies Apotropaic rites (touching of ears and nose, anointings of chest and back) Renunciation (tied to the anointings in Leidrad) includes some reference to the symbol
4) The Water Rite	
5) The Explanatory Rites	Anointing with Chrism (Signing on the forehead by the bishop) - only in Leidrad Vesting (except in K38) (perhaps including the veil)
6) Communion	
7) Other Rites	Laying on of the hand by the bishop (Odilbert and K38) Christian living

4. Type Four.

Two documents make up type four, that of Amalarius of Trier (K23) and Jessie of Amiens (K30). The liturgy they describe is taken from a Roman *ordo* for baptism, but it has become intermingled with local usages.

A. The catechumente (Q01 & Q02) and scrutinies (Q03).

These responses begin with the discussion on the reason for the catechumenate. For Amalarius the reason goes back to original sin, which makes us long for evil, and in fact makes it impossible for us to ask for baptism. For

132

anyone who comes to the church then, "necesse est ut instruatur a doctoribus ecclesiae qualis ante baptismum sit, qualis baptismum futurus sit per Dei gratiam...."[31] For Jessie the reasons are more didactic; catechumens are hearers or students.

In Amalarius and Jessie we see the full flowering of the Roman scrutiny system. They cite *OR XI* explicitly in this regard, and Amalarius mentions the fact that there are seven scrutinies as a sign of perfection, as well as the presence of the signing of the cross by the acolytes, godparents and presbyters. This rite seems to be of special importance for Amalarius who spends two entire paragraphs on this gesture.[32] The presence of genuflexions and the teaching of the Lord's prayer and the symbol (Q04 & Q05) as is found in the *Gelasianum* and in *OR XI* complete the Roman picture. Amalarius makes passing reference to what may be the renunciation of Satan (Q06), simply called the *adiurationem*, but it is not clear if this is the formal renunciation or one of a series.[33]

B. The exorcistic rites (Q08-Q10).

The exorcistic rites follow, and are still part of this single phase of the catechumenate. The order in Amalarius places the exorcism first (Q09), followed by the exsufflation (Q08) and the salt (Q10).[34] Amalarius, although he clearly preserves the anti-demonic attitude in the exorcism, does not indicate that anything is being blown out by the exsufflation. Rather it is a sign of contempt: "Exsufflatur itaque, quia tali dignus est ignominia desertor antiquus."[35] The giving

[31]Hanssens, *Amalarii*, vol. 1, p. 237, lines 25-26.

[32]Ibid., p.239: "Cur in fronte faciamus signum," and "Quali signo signemus nos."

[33]Ibid., p. 238, lines 21-23. More than one reference to a renunciation is also found in text K38.

[34]Ibid., p. 243, line 15 - p. 244, line 3.

[35]Ibid., p. 243, lines 20-21.

of the salt quotes a prayer found in the *Hadrianaum*[36] and in general speaks of the rite in terms of acquired wisdom.

Jessie places the salt first, followed by the exorcism which has the interesting title of "Exorcizatur, sive catechizatur infans,"[37] and the breathing rite. The exsufflation has the same meaning as in Amalarius, described as a sign of disdain for the devil, a sign of contempt which endures in many societies today. Perhaps this is what Jessie feels the infants need to learn. In Amalarius the giving of the salt follows, and begins with a rather odd turn of phrase for the context, "In ipso scrutinio...."[38] The last reference to a scrutiny in the singular was at the beginning of the scrutiny system, before the discussion of the seven scrutinies. Two possibilities are offered here. Either Amalarius is referring to the two immediately preceding rites, or else everything up to this point is done in the first scrutiny. The second option is grammatically more correct, which would mean that the other five scrutinies attested to by Amalarius before the seventh become either a blank space or repetitions of the same scrutiny, as is seen in *OR XI*.[39] This seems all the more likely when the sentence following the giving of the salt speaks of the intervening time for catechesis. The ordering in the work of Jessie seems to confirm this format. It is in the course of these scrutinies that Amalarius inserts the discussion of the symbol of faith and the Lord's prayer. Amalarius evidently preserves the Roman practice of celebrating these rites before Holy Saturday, since they come before the discussion of the seventh scrutiny.

---

[36]Deshusses, ed., *Hadrianum*, p. 180, no. 356. Mohlberg, Eizenhöfer, Siffrin eds., *Gelasianum*, 3rd Ed. (p. 42, no. 285) has a similar prayer, but the incipit adds the words *Pater domini nostri Iesu Christi*.

[37]*PL*, vol. 105, col. 786.

[38]Hanssens, *Amalarii*, vol. 1, p. 243, line 23.

[39]The repetition in *OR XI* is for the second (p. 426, no. 38 in the edition of Andrieu), fourth (p. 441, no. 77), fifth and sixth scrutiny (p. 442, nos. 79-80), while in this case the first five would be the same.

C. The time of year.

In the establishment of the seventh scrutiny on Holy Saturday, Amalarius gives an indication of the timing of baptism. Jessie, while citing his version of *Ordo XI* makes reference to the weeks of Lent. Apart from these two documents, only the anonymous text K50 makes reference to a specific time of year.

D. The apotropaic rites (Q11-Q14).

The apotropaic rites are held on Holy Saturday, with the touching of the nose (Q11) and ears and the anointings (Q12 - Q14). In Amalarius the touching of the nose is quite usual, but the touching of the ears is somewhat unclear, since it refers not only to the ears, but to the words coming from the mouth of the presbyter. It repeats the reference concerning the drawing of breath and then goes on to speak of the good odor we are for God. Amalarius goes on to give a second version. This seems to indicate that at least for Amalarius the touching of the ears is a new concept and has not yet found its own place in the arrangement of the rites. Thus Amalarius presents a more complicated picture.[40] The apotropaic rites take place during the seventh scrutiny, which gives them a stronger anti-demonic stress, while the touching of the nose, to which is added the touching of the ears and the *effeta*, is clearly concerned with keeping the person in the knowledge of the faith. The anointings seem to take on a more exorcistic role, being associated (as in the *Gelasianum*) with the renunciation of Satan. Still, even in this setting, the apotropaic sense remains, with a citation of Gregory the Great to indicate that the oil signifies mercy, and that the anointing on the shoulders or arms is for the taking up of and perseverence in good works. In this case the ambiguity of the Latin word *scapulae* (which can mean either back or shoulders) is resolved. Amalarius means shoulders, or even the upper arm, since this is the home of strength. In Jessie the shoulders are also indicated by the fact that the arms are

---

[40]Hanssens, *Amalarii*, vol. 1, p. 244, line 8 - p. 245, line 10.

mentioned separately.[41] Thus the anointing is for strength in good works, and both anointings direct the person to works of love, with no anti-demonic references. This presents a picture in which the bishop would be saying one thing concerning the renunciation, while doing another concerning the mercy of God and perseverence in good works, thus taking on both types of symbolism associated with these rites. In such an organization, the likelihood is that the verbal will become the dominant understanding.

For Jessie the opening of the ears becomes the major rite of the seventh scrutiny, although he does not mention the term scrutiny at this pont, since he includes here the handing on of the four Gospels, the symbol of the faith and the Lord's prayer, moving it to this point in time as the immediate preparation for baptism. This shows that the Roman *ordo* was freely adapted, since it is precisely at this point that the citations of the *ordo* cease. It is also at this point that Jessie inserts the discussion of the *conpetentes* which is followed by a second discussion of the exorcistic rites.

E. The summary of the catechumenate.

At the end of the sections on the catechumenate Amalarius tries to summarize the rites which he has just described. This proves problematic, since the summary places the giving of the salt at the beginning followed by the exorcism, sign of the cross and a genuflexion, all exorcistic in nature. The teaching of the Lord's prayer follows and then the symbol as something taught long ago. Then come the rites of touching the nostrils and ears with spittle, the anointing and confession of faith followed by the dipping in the font. If this ritual were followed, suddenly Amalarius looks very much like a type two ritual, especially that described by Leidrad, with the exorcistic rites followed by the symbol (the Lord's prayer added) the apotropaic rites, the confession of faith and the dipping in the

---

[41]"Inter scapulas tangitur, ut consecratus humerus cum scapulis totum se subjiciat potestati Dei...." *PL*, vol. 105, col. 787.

136

font. This gives an order of rites quite different from what has gone before. The reason for this variance within the document is not clear.

    F. The water rite.

    Amalarius does not specifically deal with the baptismal rite, but immediately before the recapitulation of the catechumenate comes the testing of the Godparents, to see if they can sing the Lord's prayer and the symbol. At the end of the recap of the catechumenate is the sentence, "Sicque intigitur sacro fonte baptismatis."[42] Then at the start of the section on the anointing of the head is the phrase, "Post hoc salutare lavacrum...."[43] The verb *intigitur* seems to point to infant candidates, since only they can actually be dipped, however the word is also used by several of the documents as a translation of the Greek word for baptism.[44]

    Jessie seems to confirm this picture of the baptismal rite. Immediately before the discussion of the water rite is an extensive discussion of the importance of the symbol. Then comes the discussion of the triple immersion, which covers much the same ground as Amalarius, but has this most revealing sentence, "Abrenuntiatis operibus diaboli, et mysterio credulitatis accepto, mergitur infans in aqua, et baptizatur."[45] Thus the renunciation, profession of faith and water rite all form a unity. Both rituals thus suggest that the water rite is the immediate result of renouncing the devil and professing faith in God.

    Thus the following liturgical aspects can be discerned: i) the ritual is probably mostly for children, ii) it is perhaps done by dipping, iii) it is carried out at a font and iv) the meaning of the rite is at least partially washing.

---

[42]Hanssens, *Amalarii*, vol. 1, p. 246, lines 26-27.

[43]Ibid., p. 247, line 2.

[44]For example, Leidrad, *PL*, vol. 99, col. 861.

[45]*PL*, vol. 105, col. 789.

G. The post-baptismal rites (Q15-Q18).

In both documents the anointing of the head with Chrism follows baptism, in the image of Old Testament kings and priests, and Amalarius uses similar images to explain of the linen veil. For Jessie, however the veiling has an original meaning: it is a reference to the crowns from the book of Revelations.[46] Jessie does not have a section on the white garment, but rather presents the white garment and the veil as showing the image of the just. The garment and veil represent the Christian life which the newly baptized will surely live, and refers to their appearance on the last day. For Amalarius the garment becomes the sign of the presence of the Holy Spirit, not the anointing or the laying on of the hand. It is also a sign of the wedding banquet, and through a psalm reference (Ps 131/132:9) refers to the priests of God being clothed with justice.

Jessie, unlike Amalarius, gives a full discussion of a Chrismation and the laying on of the hand by the bishop, both signifying the gift of the Holy Spirit. Jessie reminds his presbyters that only he may perform these rites, even if it is allowed for the presbyters to make the post-baptismal Chrismation.

First Eucharist follows. For Amalarius it is described as Christ being received within to replace the devil who has left. For Jessie the sense is more the sustaining of the new life received in baptism. Both refer to this rite as a confirmation with the body and blood of the Lord.

In Amalarius these rites are followed by extensive discussions of infant baptism, the already cited section on suffragans and a petition of personal unworthiness, in response to the question as to whether or not Amalarius holds what he teaches.

---

[46]*PL*, vol. 105, col. 790: "Unde et in Apocalypsi, circumamicti vestimentis albis in capitibus eius coronas aureas habere dicuntur, id est: bonis operibus induti perenni memoria mentis gaudia superna quaerant."

138

H. Summary.

Table 8

Ritual of Type Four

1) Reason for the catechumenate	
2) The Catechumenate	Names inscribed Sign of the cross on the forehead Salt Dismissal Scrutiny of genuflections, signing and laying on of the hand Repeated six times Sixth scrutiny includes the handing on of the Gospels, Lord's prayer and Creed
3) The Competentes	Exorcistic rites (salt, exorcism, exsufflation in different orders for the two) Seventh Scrutiny begins for Amalarius Apotropaic rites (touching of nose and ears, anointing chest and back) Renunciation Giving the symbol in Jessie Testing of Godparents in Amalarius
4) The Water Rite	Triple immersion
5) The Explanatory Rites	Anointing with Chrism Veiling Vesting Laying on of the hand (called confirmation, only present in Jessie)
6) Communion	Also called confirmation

The liturgies described in these two places are remarkable for their strong Roman influence.   In Trier and Amiens it seems that a form of the Roman liturgy has become normative. This does not mean, however, that local variation has disappeared. The ritual is quite different as a whole from the sources which Amalarius and Jessie quoted in parts of their responses. Clearly there has been a good deal of adapting the rites to the needs of the local churches, although not so much that the general Roman structure would be lost. A picture of a ritual which is basically Roman in structure emerges.

5. Hybrids.

Three documents represent liturgies which fall within the general scope of the four types described above, but have significant variations which seem to place them in more than one of the types. These three documents, K12, K50 and K53 are also sufficiently different from each other, and so will not be described as a type of ritual, but rather will be discussed in terms of how they relate to the main types.

A. The first rites.

The catechumenate which begins texts K53 and K12 is a time of instruction, even in the case of infants. K12 begins with an extensive section of definitions, which gives the impression of being a brief catechesis. In K53 the reason for the catechumenate is linked to the possibility of damnation, "Animae quoque suae immortalitatem et aeternam sanctis gloriam; malis vero aeterna tormenta pro meritorum qualitate audiens credat, retribuenda fore."[47] It is no surprise then that this period begins with the scrutiny (Q03), in the fashion of types one and four. Unlike type one, however, the discussion of the symbol does not follow the scrutiny. The reference to the scrutiny is again in the singular.

The beginning of K50 is also much like type one, in that the catechesis, scrutiny and discussion of the symbol all precede the exorcistic rites. The whole rite begins, however, with the Roman elements of the giving of the name, the

---

[47]*PL*, vol. 98, col. 938.

140

signing with the cross[48] and the giving of the salt, which is not seen in exorcistic terms, but more as an opening to the wisdom of God. These elements make this text seem more like a type four document.

B. The exorcistic rites (Q08-Q10).

In K53 these rites are in the usual order for type one rituals: exsufflation (Q08), exorcism (Q09), salt (Q10). All three rites are anti-demonic. The giving of the salt, even though it is called the *condimentum sapientiae*,[49] is to take away the sins of the person. The exorcism is in the name of the eternal God and the exsufflation for the removal of spirits. The references to the Father in the first, to spirits in the second and to wisdom in the third of these rites seem to invoke each person of the Trinity in turn. The order in K12 is exsufflation, the giving of salt, exorcism, the receiving of salt. With the exorcism in the midst of the salt rite, it could be an exorcism of the salt, which is alluded to in other documents (for example K50[50]). However the exorcism is equally applicable to the person, being very like the description of the exorcism in many of the other documents, "Hoc est coniuratus malignus spiritus, ut exeat aet recedat, dans locum Deo vero."[51] In K50 the exorcistic rites are spread throughout the ritual, with the salt in the beginning, the exorcism following the discussion of the symbol and the exsufflation following the apotropaic rites, the only text which has any exorcistic rites following the apotropaic ones. Apart from this innovation these two follow the

---

[48]Explained in terms of the Israelites putting a sign upon their doors in the Exodus Event: "Et bene prius signantur quam baptizentur, quia prius postes filiorum Israel agni sanguine signantur quam mare rubrum transeant, per quod significatur baptismatis sacramentum." Wilmart, "Une catéchèse baptismale," p. 196.

[49]*PL*, vol. 98, col. 938.

[50]Wilmart, "Une catéchèse baptismale," p. 196, "...sal exorcizatum ac benedictum...."

[51]Vogel, *Le pontifical*, p. 173, lines 16-17.

type one liturgies, being followed immediately by the apotropaic rites. Text K53 follows types two and three, placing the discussion of the symbol after the exorcistic rites.

C. The *traditio symboli,* renunciation and adherence (Q04-Q05, Q06-Q07).

Text K50 has long since finished with the discussion of the symbol, having placed it at the beginning of the catechumenate as in type one. The renunciation is kept until just before the baptism, linking the renunciation of sin to the water rite through images of the flood and the crossing of the sea, "Notandum uero quod et in arca Noe et in transitu maris rubri baptismatis sacramentum praefiguratum fuit."[52] Document K12 places both the symbol and the renunciation (in that order) immediately before the water rite. Text K53 has the giving of the symbol after the exorcistic rites. It is described as the decoration for the house of God which the person is about to become. The author of this response had obviously read the mind of the emperor concerning the circular letter, since the description of the symbol which follows takes up a third of the response. The renunciation of Satan is intimately associated with the handing on of the symbol. But it is worthy of note that the discussion of the new faith is given first, before the discussion of the renunciation in both this document and K12. Could it be that the symbol is given in order to make the renunciation possible? The sentence following the renunciation clouds the issue, and may indicate that the renunciation is ritually first, "Quibus omnibus abdicatis, tota spes in solum Deum ponenda est."[53]

---

[52]Wilmart, "Une catéchèse baptismale," p. 200.

[53]*PL,* vol. 98, col. 939.

142

D. The apotropaic rites (Q12 - Q14).

The apotropaic rites in K53 are as follows: the nose and ears are signed with spittle, with a generic Gospel allusion to spittle coming from the mouth of the Lord,[54] but the rite has a pneumatological sense, associated with the drawing of breath (*spiritus*), and an encouragement to have spiritual ears. In K50 the rites of touching the ears and nose are placed in the midst of two exorcistic rites, a structure not seen elsewhere. This is followed by the renunciation of Satan. In K12 the touching follows the exorcistic rites, as in type one documents, but is followed by the renunciation and the discussion of the symbol as in types three and four. An additional sense is given to these rites, which makes them an icon of the participation of the Son in the essence of the Father, since spittle comes from the head, and the head of Christ is God (1Cor 11:3).[55]

In K53 the anointing of the chest with a sign of the cross is seen as a protection against a return of the devil. The signing of the back or shoulders is seen as a celebration of the freedom of having renounced the yoke of slavery of the devil and anointed as free children of God. For K12 the anointings follow the touchings, but in K50 the exsufflation intervenes, as does a discussion of the reason why Chrism is consecrated on Holy Thursday. The Chrism is said to be used on Easter, when the church baptizes, providing the only other indication of when the baptismal ritual would take place apart from Amalarius and Jessie. The anointing then follows, with an additional anointing in front with Chrism, which is given the same sense as the post-baptismal Chrismation in many of the other responses, that of the royal priesthood. That this should occur before the water rite is very interesting, but is not a transposition, since the post-baptismal anointing

---

[54]Ibid.: "quia legimus sputum quod de capite Domini processit, gratiam Spiritus sancti designari...."

[55]Vogel, *Le pontifical*, p. 173, lines 23-25: "...quia sicut sputum de iterioribus capitis procedit, ita filius de substantia patris nascitur, cum dicit apostolus: *Caput Christi Deus.*"

is described in a separate sentence at the appropriate point in the ritual.

E. The renunciation and water rite.

Texts K12 and K50 both place the renunciation of Satan at this point, in direct relationship with the water rite. In text K50 the renunciation and water rite are considered in the same sentence. Text K12 is alone in placing the discussion of the symbol at this point, but it is seen as part of the renunciation, which in turn leads to the water rite. This is similar in style to types three and four.

The water rite in text K12 is much more extensive. The text discusses the meaning of the word *baptism* as well as the form, "Post haec baptizatur in aqua his verbis: *In nomine patris et filii et spiritus sancti.*"[56] This is followed by a discussion on the meaning of the Trinity as three and yet one, and then an expansion on the *Primo paganus* text concerning death by the third step of sin. All the other texts that cite this passage give only the third step, consent, but this text includes all three steps, "consensu, suasione et delectatione...."[57] referring to the steps which led to the fall of Adam and Eve.

The discussion of the water rite in text K53 briefly mentions the immersion in the image of the Trinity, followed by the reference from *Primo paganus* to the third grade of sin. The same elements appear as seen above: baptism is in the name of the Trinity, by triple immersion and perhaps in a font that has three steps.

F. The post-baptismal rites (Q15 - Q18).

These rites are dealt with in short order in texts K53 and K12, following *Primo paganus*, with one minor alteration: K53 adds *solemnitatem* to the joy of regeneration at the vesting. The order of the rites is in typical type one fashion, although this order has also been seen in text K38 of type two. The laying on of the hand of the bishop follows, as the gift of the Spirit. Text K12 makes two

---

[56]C. Vogel, *Le pontifical*, p. 174, number 16, line 22.

[57]Ibid,. p. 175, number 17, lines 1-2.

amendments to the text. First it has a second reason for the white garment, that of a sign of the immortality lost by Adam which is regained in baptism. Second is a reference to the passion and resurrection in the passage on first Eucharist. The question on the laying on of the hand is also unusual, since it does not ask why the hand is laid, but why the bishop does not lay the hand on catechumens before now, the answer being the quote from *Primo paganus* which indicates that the bishop gives the gift of the Spirit.

G. Conclusion.

These rituals are clearly hybrids. While they have many of the elements of a type one ritual, they also have much which places them in the category of types three and four. The task of placing rituals into specific types is not a simple task, and even the meaning of individual rites within specific descriptions is not always clear. Thus it seems best not to force the issue and rather allow for a less rigid division between the ritual types, since that is what the evidence suggests.

6. Type Five: Aquileia.

The case of the response of Maxentius was identified as a type unto itself. Apart from what is known about the diocese and its liturgy, the ritual was set aside because the beginning of the *conpetentes* is found before the exorcistic rites, the only ritual to do so. It is also the only one to place the giving of the salt as the first of the exorcistic rites, and has almost no reference to a pre-baptismal anointing. Finally it has in common with the circular letter an absence of any reference to the laying on of the hand of the bishop.

A. The catechumenate (Q01 & Q02).

The beginning of the catechumenate is the start of a period of study, but the rite is not described. What is certain is that it is not the confession of faith, since this is the place that the catechumen desires to be and is hastening to achieve.

B. *Conpetentes.*

The *conpetentes* pose a problem. On one hand the text indicates that the catechumens can also be called *conpetentes*. But on the other, *conpetentes* are those who have already accepted the faith, which does not fit the description of the catechumens given in the previous sentence. *Conpetentes* are those who are asking for the grace of God.

C. Exorcistic rites.

The giving of salt (Q10) is included with the exorcistic ministry, but is not exorcistic in itself, referring rather to the scriptures "...Vos estis sal terræ...."[58] The rite for the giving of the salt indicates that it has the sense of granting the wisdom of God, as was seen in the response of Magnus. The exorcism (Q09) and exsufflation (Q08) appear to be one and the same, and are seen in the usual sense, although Maxentius makes a creative allusion to the strong man who must be tied up before his goods can be plundered (Matt 12:29), evidently equating the strong man with the devil. For Maxentius the antidemonic aspect is much less emphasized, to the point where the word Satan does not even appear. The formula for the giving of the salt is the same as in the *Gelasianum*,[59] and it is salt for wisdom and as medicine for eternal salvation. The exorcism and exsufflation which follow are dealt with as one act and refer to the prince of this world who is driven out, who is not a creature of God.

D. The scrutiny (Q03).

It is only at this point that the term scrutiny arises, and it is described only in general terms as including prayers of priests in the plural, a laying on of the hand followed by some form of anointing of the body to prepare it for the dwelling of the Holy Spirit. These rites seem to require more than one priest, but the laying on

---

[58]*PL*, vol. 106, col. 51, see Matt 5:13.

[59]Mohlberg, Eizenhöfer, Siffrin, eds., *Gelasianum*, 3rd ed., no. 289, p. 43.

146

of the hand remains in the singular. The rites of prayer and the laying on of the hand have an exorcistic nature. The anointing which follows is the only reference to any of what are the apotropaic rites in all the other documents studied. In this case, however, the emphasis is on preparing a place for God, a temple for the Spirit. For Maxentius there are no separate apotropaic rites. This is to be expected in Aquileia, where even the exorcistic group of rites has lost its strong anti-demonic sense and been adapted to a more apotropaic nature.

E. The renunciation of Satan (Q06-Q07) and the water rite.

The renunciation is placed in the context of the taking off of the old person and putting on the new (Eph 4:21, 24). The renunciation is associated in this case with the water rite, with the removal of the old clothes to enter the font, and the vesting with the white garment.

The water rite is briefly described, and involves the entry into the font (which may refer to the baptistry rather than the font itself) and a triple immersion in the name of the Trinity. This indicates the following: i) baptism by immersion; ii) a triple immersion; iii) baptism in the name of the Trinity; and iv) either a font large enough to enter or a baptistry. There follows an almost rubrical comment, "deinde translati ad gremium matris Ecclesiæ,"[60] which may describe a ritual as well as theological reality.

F. The post-baptismal rites (Q15-Q17).

In the response of Maxentius the post-baptismal rites have this arrangement: First comes the anointing with Chrism, and the text indicates the whole body is anointed, not just the head. This would explain the reason why both garments are put on after the anointing, as opposed to only the Chrismal veil, which has been the norm. The vesting of the neophytes is couched in eschatological terms, as preparation for entering the eternal promised land and the heavenly banquet. These references have obvious Eucharistic overtones. The

---

[60]*PL*, vol. 106, col. 52.

Eucharist may also be behind the placement of the explanation of the symbol. H. Boone Porter has already shown that this document testifies to the *traditio symboli* of the North Italian churches.[61] The placement of the discussion of the symbol at this point would indicate a *redditio symboli* not before but after the baptismal rite. This is very unlikely. It is much more probable that this is the creed of the baptismal Eucharist, which Dix asserts was introduced at Aquileia by the Patriarch Paul II (786-802).[62]

G. First Eucharist (Q18).

In keeping with Maxentius' style, the description of first Eucharist is made up of scriptural references, all from the sixth chapter of the Gospel of John. This is clearly the completion of the rites of initiation, since the last citation has Christ promising to remain in those who eat his flesh and drink his blood (John 6:55-56).

H. Summary:

Maxentius presents a baptismal liturgy which, while it has some of the aspects of a Roman rite, is clearly of a separate type.

[61]See H. B. Porter, "Maxentius of Aquileia," pp. 3-9.

[62]Dix, *Shape*, p. 487, based upon an article by B. Cappelle, "L'origine antiadoptianiste de notre texte du Symbole de la Messe," *Recherches de théologie ancienne et médievale*, 1(1929): 19-20: "L'actif ouvrier de cette oeuvre fut Paulin d'Aquilée, en qui l'on doit reconnaître l'auteur de la version latine du Symbole encore en usage aujourd'hui."

148

Table 9

Ritual of Type Five

1) Catechumenate	Instruction
2) *Competentes*	Exorcistic rites (salt; exorcism and exsufflation together) Scrutiny (prayer and laying on of the hand, anointing) Renunciation
3) Water Rite	
4) Explanatory Rites	Anointing with Chrism Vesting Veiling
5) Communion	
6) Creed	

7. Conclusions.

At the end of this chapter three things can be said. First is that the types established in the last chapter by the ordering of the rites within the ritual seem to hold firm under this closer examination. There is a basic unity of structure within the types with more than one representative, and structures separate each of the types from the others.

Second, there is room within these divisions for a certain latitude. Within this basic unity of form and content there are shades of emphasis which blur the lines between the different ritual types. What we are dealing with here is more of a rainbow, with differences within the ritual types giving shadings of meaning. The relative clarity of the descriptions allows the postulation of this gradation of rituals.

A third conclusion is that there are certain blocks of rites within a ritual which are always found together, and generally have a certain unity of purpose. These have been identified as apotropaic, exorcistic and post-baptismal rites.

These titles have been used without question to this point. The next chapter will examine the veracity of these titles.

The Table which follows compares the rituals in general terms, which allows us to see more clearly the similarities and differences.

Table 10

Comparison of the Rituals

Type One	Type Two	Type Three	Type Four	Type Five
Enter Catechumenate	*Enter Catechumenate*			
Catechumenate	(Renunciation)	*Catechumenate*	*Catechumenate*	*Catechumenate*
Scrutiny one/more	Exorcistics exsufflation, exorcism, salt	Exorcistics (exorcism, exsufflation, salt) (anointing)	Give Names	
Symbol	*Catechumenate*		Sign w/cross	
Renunciation	Symbol		Salt	
Exorcistics exsufflation, exorcism, salt	Scrutiny		Dismissal	
			Scrutinies (7)	
			Gospels,	
			Lord's prayer, Creed	
		Competentes	*Competentes*	*Competentes*
		Symbol	Exorcistics: salt, exorcism/exsufflation	Exorcistics
		Scrutinies	Apotropaic rites (touch nose and ears anoint chest & back)	salt
Apotropaic rites touch of nose & other parts anoint chest & back	Apotropaic rites touch nose and ears anoint chest & back	Apotropaic rites (touch ears and nose, anoint chest & back)	Renunciation	exorcism
		Renunciation	Symbol	exsufflation
				Scrutiny
				Renunciation
Water Rite	*Water Rite*	*Water Rite*	*Water Rite*	*Water Rite*
Explanatory Rites	*Explanatory Rites*	*Explanatory Rites*	*Explanatory Rites*	*Explanatory Rites*
Vesting	Vesting	Chrism	Chrism	Chrism
Chrism	Chrism	(Signing forehead)	Veiling	Vesting
Veiling	Veiling	Vesting	Vesting	Veiling
		(Veiling?)	Laying on of the hand	
Communion	*Communion*	*Communion*	*Communion*	*Communion*
Other Rite	*Other Rite*	*Other Rite*		Creed
Laying on of the hand	Laying on of the hand	Laying on of hand		

CHAPTER SIX

THE BAPTISMAL LITURGY OF THE EMPIRE

TYPES AND THEOLOGY

1. Introduction.

Christian initiation, or "christening," is the process which a person
goes through while being transformed into a new creation,
modelled in the likeness of Christ himself. The sacraments of
initiation mark the stages of that transformation and help to bring it
about.[1]

In the previous chapter the documents included in this study were
examined and were found to fall into a number of types. The purpose of this
chapter is compare these five types of baptismal liturgy as well as the hybrids
between them and to begin to examine them theologically. We have seen in the
analysis of the documents a number of liturgical blocks, namely the entry into the
catechumenate, the apotropaic rites, those which are more exorcistic in nature,
those associated with the *traditio* of the symbol of faith and the post-baptismal
rites. These blocks of rites will be discussed in turn. In addition there were two
rites, the scrutiny and the renunciation, which seem to have been placed
independently. These will be discussed when they arise in their relationship with
the main liturgical blocks.

First Eucharist and the role of the bishop will be discussed with the post-
baptismal rites, as their place in these rites has lasting importance for the Roman
church. The water rite itself will be treated separately because of its importance,

---

[1]M. Searle, *Christening*, p. 1.

although it is the one which received the least comment in the documents.

The rites will be examined in the following order: The entry into the catechumenate, the period of the catechumenate, the exorcistic rites, the symbol, the apotropaic rites, the water rite and finally the post-baptismal rites and communion.

The theological significance of each of the groups of rites described above will be examined and a comparison made between the different theological approaches of each of the types of baptismal liturgy.

2. The Entry into the Catechumenate.

The rites of entry into the catechumenate are described in all the responses to the circular letter except that of Maxentius of Aquileia. The sense of the individual rites vary depending upon the structure of the whole. Type one and type four documents, as well as the three hybrid documents all place the scrutiny as one of the rites of entry into the catechumenate. The scrutiny is thus not a test of faith, since the symbol has not yet been handed on. Rather the scrutiny has the sense of a teaching of the faith, especially for type one liturgies which have the handing on of the symbol with the renunciation of Satan as the entry into the catechumenate. The rites of entry into the catechumenate are here focused on the beginning of a training in the faith. The question seems to be one of testing to see if they are able to learn the faith, "...quia tunc scrutandi sunt catechumeni, si rectam jam noviter fidem symboli eis traditam firmiter teneant."[2] In all of these cases the exorcistic rites follow, but because of what has already happened, they are not the rites of entry into the catechumenate, but rather rites of purification which occur while the catechumens are in training.

For types two and three, however, this is not the case. The exorcistic rites are the rites of entry into the catechumenate. Thus the whole approach to the making of a catechumen is different. Rather than a training in the matters of faith,

---

[2]Keefe, "An Unknown Response," p. 57, lines 31-33.

the sense is one of snatching the person from the power of the devil. For type three documents these are the only rites of the catechumenate proper, since the discussion of the *conpetentes* always follows these exorcistic rites. For Maxentius of Aquileia the rites of entry into the catechumenate are not discussed at all, but the entry into the *conpetentes* comes first, followed by the exorcistic rites.

3. The Time of Instruction.

For all but type one [and two of the hybrid documents (K12 and K50)] there exists an explicit discussion of the period of time between the exorcistic and apotropaic rites. For type three liturgies and document K30 this includes the entry into the *conpetentes*, and for all but Maxentius of Aquileia it includes the discussion of the symbol of faith. For types two, three and five this is also the time of the scrutiny. Whether these rites were part of a single celebration with the water rite as seems to be indicated by the Gallican missals,[3] or whether they still

---

[3]The *Missale Bobbiense* and the *Missale Gothicum* both include, before the beginning of the baptismal ritual proper on Holy Saturday, a vestige of the rites of entry into the catechumenate. They deserve special comment because of the way in which they are used. Lowe, *The Bobbio Missal*, p. 71, no. 232, for its part has a signing with the cross on the forehead for which this prayer is provided:

> Facis signum + in eum et dices simbolum. Accipe signum crucis
> tam in fronte quam et in corde semper esto fidelis templum dei
> ingredere idola derelinque cole deum patrem omnipotentem et iesu
> christo filium eius qui uenturus es iudicare uiuos et mortuos
> saeculum per ignem cum spirito sancto in saecula saeculorum.

Then, on the following folio of the manuscript the text continues, "Ill. accipe spiritum sanctum in cor retenias." which is preceded by the rubric "Post hec insufflabis in os eius ter et dices." [Lowe, *The Bobbio Missal*, p. 73, no. 233]. The other source, L.C. Mohlberg, ed., *Missale Gothicum (Vat. Reg. Lat. 317)*, Rerum Ecclesiasticarum Documenta, Series Maior, Fontes, vol. 5 (Rome: Herder, 1961), pp. 65-66, nos. 253-254, appears to give two prayers for the signing:

> ITEM COLLECTIO. Accipe signaculum Christi, suscipe uerba
> diuina, inluminare uerbum domini, quia hodie confessus es a

154

required an interval of time at least as long as Lent to complete them, the rites of the scrutiny and the handing on of the faith still have a very different function than that found in the type one liturgies. Here the symbol is not the key to enter the school of faith, but rather is the curriculum for that school. For type three and four documents as well as the hybrid document K12, there is a testing on this curriculum immediately before the water rite itself.

In cases where infants are being baptized, this period of catechesis may seem even more difficult to understand, since the profession is not made by the children. For the respondents to the circular letter, however, this does not seem to be a difficulty, since in those places near the centre of the empire, such as the type one liturgies represent, this teaching of the faith is still given the first place of importance.

4. The Exorcistic Rites.

From what we have seen exorcistic rites were an important part of the catecheumenate. "The ceremonies which accompanied the admission to the simple catechumenate in the ranks of the *audientes* or *auditores* were all centered around

---

Christo: per dominum.
ITEM COLLECTIO. Signo te in nomine patris et filii et spiritus sancti, ut sis christianus; oculos, ut uideas claritatem dei, aures, ut audias uocem domini, nares, ut odoris suauitatem Chrisi, <linguam> conuersus ut confitearis patrem et filium et spiritum sacntum, cor, ut credas trinitatem inseparabilem. Pax tecum: per Iesum Christum dominum nostrum, qui cum patre [et filio] et spiritu sancto uiuit.

Both documents show only the last remnants of this signing, which once marked the entry into the catechumenate. Still they are instructive, since they show that this act was understood in both a pneumatological and a Christological sense. P. de Puniet sees this signing with the cross on the forehead as the most long-lasting of all the ceremonies of the catechumenate. Their presence here is an indication that the rites were preserved even after the disappearance of a functioning catechumenate.

the theme of liberation from Satan and the way now opened to Christ."[4]

All the documents mention an exorcism at least once and the associated rites have included the giving of the salt and the exsufflation or insufflation. Of these three rites the exorcism itself is clearest in its meaning, with the exsufflation and the salt often having different meanings. Of the three exorcistic rites the salt is the least exorcistic in nature and seems in many cases to be a bridge between the exorcistic and apotropaic rites of the catechumenate. Just what is being exorcised or breathed out or salted away varies considerably, which shows that the power of the devil was not always central to these rites.

Type four documents, as well as text K38 and the hybrid text K50 have a second time of exorcism. This usually comes before the apotropaic rites, although text K50 associates it with the apotropaic rites. In the exorcistic rites there is a set of theologies, not a single vision. This is somewhat surprising in a set of rites which would seem to be fairly clear in their meaning, especially the exorcism. What we see instead is a variety of world views being expressed in the rites of exorcism. For example in Leidrad, the titanic struggle of salvation is clear, there is good and evil, and the good must be victorious over the evil one. In the section on baptism, where he refers to the *arena hujus mundi* and then clearly to the two adversaries and their supporters: "Utramque enim partem, Christi scilicet et diaboli, infinita populi multitudo spectat luctantem."[5] Clearly the struggle is between Christ and the devil. This may seem obvious, but it is not, since in

[4]C. Vagaggini, *Theological Dimensions of the Liturgy: A General Treatise on the Theology of the Liturgy*, L. Doyle, W. Jurgens, trans. from the 4th Italian ed. (Collegeville, MN: Liturgical Press, 1976), pp. 397-398.

[5]*PL*, vol. 99, col. 861.

156

Maxentius[6] and Magnus[7] and Amalarius[8] the struggle is between the person being baptized, not Christ, and the evil spirit, and Christ is invited in only after the battle is all but done. This is an enormous difference, and one that is not immediately clear. If Jesus Christ, ruler of the universe, is still in pitched battle with Satan, Lord of darkness, then the world and all that is in it is truly in peril. The victory of the cross is, if not absent, then at least not as definitive as one might hope. In a world where superstition, mysterious diseases and witchcraft lived and in a society which was within reach of those who were considered agents of the devil, the Saracens, such a world-view would have made sense and would have met the needs of the people. For the other three types, however, the participants in the struggle have changed. There is an enemy, but Christ himself need not be called out. Any priest is sufficient to beat back the force which we inherited because of that unfortunate incident in Eden. A breath and a few words are all that are required; in Amalarius even the breath loses its active role and rather indicates the power of people to hold Satan in contempt.

It is therefore not possible to reduce the meaning of these rites to a single image. At least two different world views are found in these exorcistic rites. Still the appellation of exorcism is correct; it simply reflects different attitudes to the removal of the power of Satan from the person.

---

[6]*PL*, vol. 106, col. 52.

[7]Keefe, "An Unknown Response," p. 58, lines 62-64, "Insufflantur etenim qui baptizandi sunt a Dei sacerdote ut ex eis princeps effugetur peccatorum...."

[8]The breathing rite described above makes this clear.

5. The Symbol.

In all the responses the symbol of faith is of extreme importance.[9] Several of them cite the entire symbol in the course of their reflections. But in the different types, there are different approaches to its placement and exact purpose.

There are four different approaches to the placement of the symbol within the rites. As we have seen in type one the symbol is the entry to the catechumenate, the ritual sign that the person is now on the way to salvation. In types two and three the symbol is the content of the school of faith, which one needs to master in order to proceed to the font. In type four the curriculum is broadened with the addition of the teaching of the Lord's prayer and Gospels. In addition there is a second ritual in which the symbol is either handed on again or in which the godparents are tested immediately before baptism, so that the symbol becomes the key not to the catechumenate, but rather to the font. In the case of

---

[9]The term *symbol* has been used from the outset of this work. In the discussion of the meaning of the symbol of faith within the baptismal rite, it is important to have an understanding of why such a term was used for the creed in the first place.

The following is synthesized and quoted from the article by H.J. Carpenter, "*Symbolum* as a Title of the Creed," in *Journal of Theological Studies*, first series, 43 (1942): 1-11.

The first use in the Greek of the term comes from the council of Laodicea (343-381), but the term was not commonly used until the fifth century. "It seems therefore certain that the title originated in the West, and that it is the meaning of *symbolum* rather than το συμβολον that we have to trace back to its origin." p. 3

The term appears in twice Tertullian, once in his tract against Marcion and a second time in reference to baptism. Both times it has a legal interpretation, and it is the baptismal reference that interests us. It has here the sense of a "written document or bond which would demand our death as the stipulated penalty for our sins if God did not make us a present of it in baptism." p.4 This legal use thus comes from Roman society.

Later Christian writers will see the term as referring to "a covenant or pact of which the substance is faith in the threefold Name and which is made formal and binding by the interrogations, responses, and triple immersion." p. 9 This is the sense often found in the documents of this study. Still, the original meaning of a pardon by the gracious act of God is not inconsistent with this later sense, and in fact gives it a nuance which helps us to better understand its meaning.

Maxentius, the symbol has a mysterious placement, at the end of the ritual, a placement for which there is no certain explanation. What is strange is that the emperor, in receiving these missives, let alone the others of which we are aware, did not seem at all perturbed by this great variance at the heart of the baptismal ritual, in what was for him far and away the most important section. It seems the emperor was just glad to know there was no evidence of heresy and that there were rituals of sufficient solemnity to hand on these articles of faith. From this evidence, it seems he was not particularly concerned with how it was done, so long as it was done.

6. The Apotropaic Rites.

In the descriptions of the various types, it has become clear that the apotropaic rites have a more nebulous quality. In type one liturgies they are clearly apotropaic in nature. The exorcisms precede these rites and lead immediately to the water rite. Thus they are the final strengthening needed to prevent the return of the devil at this most critical of moments. In types two, three and four, however, the meaning is partially usurped by a need for more exorcism. These types have other rites between the exorcistic rites and the apotropaic rites, often the scrutiny and the rites concerning the symbol of faith. Types three and four also insert the renunciation and confession of faith between these rites and the water rite. The general sense is that there needs to be a greater amount of testing of the candidate. For those in type one, the single exorcism is sufficient, and the apotropaic rites retain their meaning. When other rites intervene or follow, however, there is a second moment of testing, immediately before the water rite. These two approaches reveal a different conception of the catechumenate, a difference which is reflected in the different senses given to the apotropaic rites. In the case of type one liturgies, the sense is that the entry into the catechumenate is completed by an exorcism, one which will have no need of repetition. The other types discussed to this point present a different perspective, one in which the entry into the catechumenate and the exorcism is not in itself sufficient to cleanse a person from evil. In these types the entire complex of the catechumenate is exorcistic.

In a third approach (Maxentius) the apotropaic rites are all but non-existent, with the exorcistic rites taking on the apotropaic functions. Here the sense is more a question of entering into the heart of the church, of being held and sustained by the rites of the *conpetentes*.

7. The Water Rite.

The question of the water rite does not form part of the circular letter, but since it is the heart of the ritual and was discussed in several of the responses, it will be briefly examined here.

Some of the texts, like the circular letter, do not mention the water rite at all. Those that do mention it all witness to a triple immersion. Leidrad does refer to the practice of single immersion, but only as something which is done elsewhere. The water rite is seen as the washing away of sin, as the death and rebirth of the person in Christ, and in some cases, such as Maxentius, as a clear entry into the church. The lack of variety in the understanding of this rite is not surprising. As the heart of the rite, its meaning remains constant, even as the ordering and meaning of the preparatory and subsequent rites develop.

8. The Post-Baptismal Rites.

The post-baptismal rites are very important for understanding the meaning of the whole ritual. In essence these rites tell us who a Christian is and what baptism has done. They are explanatory rites, and the authors of the documents clearly see them in this light.

Of all the types, the Aquileian liturgy has the most eschatological view of the post-baptismal rites. Maxentius sees all that happens after the water rite as celebrating the entry into the fulness of the kingdom of God. Nowhere else is the Book of Revelations and the blood of the lamb so emphasized. For him, these rites are intended to explain what has just happened: the person has entered into the eternal life of the kingdom. There is no doubt about the future, death will come, but will be welcomed, since the baptized one is already a citizen of heaven, having been anointed unto eternal life, clothed with the garment of the just and fed on the food of heaven.

This sense is much less evident, although never completely absent in the other types. Type three liturgies generally see these rites in terms of Old Testament figures and in terms of the responsibilities and privileges of this life. It seems that the laying on of the hand, with the goal of preaching to others, has changed the dynamic of these rites, greatly reducing their significance in terms of heavenly citizenship.

The references to first Eucharist likewise generally look backwards to the last supper rather than forwards to the end of time and the heavenly banquet. The general attitude to first Eucharist is that one should partake of the body of which one is a member, that one should receive the food which nourishes the soul so as not to go spiritually hungry. Attacks are evidently already being made on infant communion: the reasoning concerning the integrity of the body will encourage infant communion, and in fact remains an excellent argument for our own day.

9. Conclusion.

This analysis has shown that the liturgies described by the various types have different theological emphases. Some, such as type five (Maxentius) reveal a strong eschatology, particularly in the post-baptismal rites. Others present the symbol of faith as the way of entry into the faith, and the catechumenate as the school of faith or the time to fully drive the devil away. Each has its own internal rhythm, and each type with more than one document has shown a certain variety within that type. Still, the types each present the same faith and understanding of the reason for baptism.

CONCLUSIONS

1. The Empire and its Church.

The study of the circular letter and responses has revealed a growing empire and church. The metropolitan system of governance of the church is not firmly established, but is in the process of developing. The empire too, even though the emperor is at the end of his reign, is still in the process of being defined, certainly in terms of geography, but also in terms of the relation with the papacy and the Eastern empire based in Constantinople. Alcuin, now dead, has had a profound influence upon many of the bishops currently in place, having trained many of them. The importance that liturgy appears to have in the empire is surely the result, in part, of his influence. It will not endure into the era that is to come.

2. Liturgy and Charlemagne.

Partly as a result of this understanding of the church and the empire, but also from the study of the circular letter and responses, it is no longer possible to attribute to Charlemagne the strong Romanization policy mentioned as a matter of course in scholarly work. There is no evidence in these documents of an attempt to enforce a unified ritual or in fact a single mode of celebration. The responses in their great variety show that the details of individual rites were not celebrated in a uniform way. What mattered was teaching and proper celebration, so that the people entrusted to emperor's leadership would be brought to God. There were any number of ways in which one might follow the Romans without a line by line accord, or even an identical ordering of elements within the ritual. This conclusion gives a better understanding of the meaning of the communion these churches had with Rome.

3. The Types of Baptismal Liturgy.

This study has also shown that there continued to exist a family of rituals. One part of this study has been to take the rituals as described by the responses and attempt to classify them. There was some success in this endeavor, but it must also be admitted that the types of rituals blend into each other. There are certainly similarities in the types of rituals, but when taken together all five types had specific aspects which were considered essential, which could not be reduced to a single ritual. This is even more clearly shown by those documents which did not fit within the categories established by this study. Each type had a different theological emphasis when the representatives of the types were submitted to closer examination. It is important to see these for what they were: local rituals. The expression of the culture, the climate, the temperament of the people and other variables all must have figured into the way in which the people celebrated these rites.

4. The Church.

The consequence of the study of the documents of the time, together with the study of the relationship between church and empire, is an appreciation of the development which the church underwent at this time. To find such a large body of work on baptism (even if much of it was initiated at the behest of the emperor) all grouped in a short space of time indicates that the church had to spend a good deal of time in thought and prayer on baptism. This return to basics revealed the vitality and variety of expression which the Carolingian line fostered. The study of the documents has also shown this church to have a continuity with the sources of Scripture and the Fathers, and a relatively high level of learning, at least at the level of the metropolitan archbishops.

In the same light, the rituals show a variety of theological expression, both in their overall understanding of the sacramental life of the church and in the meaning of the details of the rites.

5. Applications.

A fifth conclusion regards the future direction of scholarship and praxis. If we have been able to come to these conclusions in the light of this body of material, it is in part with a goal to use it as a base to reconsider our study of earlier centuries, for which there is much less information. It is by no means certain that a single ritual will be found at the base of all of this, in fact the opposite seems the more likely. Still it is the hope that this study will urge on the further work on these documents, as well as the larger context of baptism in this territory both before and after the year 811/812.

From a pastoral perspective, two things may be concluded: 1) The catechumenate endured into the beginning of the ninth century, at least in some parts of the empire. Where it did not survive because the candidates for initiation were mostly infants, the testing of Godparents became an option. 2) The current rite for the initiation of adults, while following the Roman system, is not the only approach used in the tradition of the Western church.

The theological differences which have been revealed by the different ordering of rites within the rituals should give food for thought to those who may, in times to come, look to a second edition of the adult initiation rites.

One of the pastoral difficulties this author has experienced is that much time in the catechumenate is spent on scrutiny and exorcistic rites, while the apotropaic rites and the *traditio symboli* and that of the Lord's prayer and Gospels are considered as lesser or even optional elements. It seems that at least in some of the documents covered in this study, these optional elements were considered at least as important as the exorcistic elements.

Finally a word should be said concerning the tradition which this study sought to examine. The circular letter and the responses have shown a wide variety of nuances concerning the way in which Christians are made, but the unity of their voice concerning the centrality of baptism in the life of the church is of

164

enduring value. We are fundamentally, after all, a people saved by God through
the waters:

> Post hæc vero ingressi fontem baptismatis, sub *trina mersione*
> baptizati in nomine Patris, et Filii, et Spiritus sancti (Matt 28:19);
> deinde translati ad gremium matris Ecclesiæ per lavacrum
> regenerationis, adoptionis filii effecti (cf Eph 1:4-5), scripti in libro
> vitæ (cf Rev 3:5, 17:8) Christi Domini nostri, a cujus sancto nomine
> *chrisma* nomen accepit, peruncti etiam hujus sacræ unctionis
> chrisma salutis, id est, sancti Spiritus largissima infusione in Christo
> Jesu, Domino nostro in vitam æternam, regenerati quoque Jesum
> ducem sequentes (cf Mt 9:9), et loti in sanguine Agni (cf Rev
> 22:14), albis induti (cf Rev 3:18), id est nuptiales vestes (cf Matt
> 32:11-12) ad mensam coelestis regni (cf Is 25:6), ad illam veram
> repromissionis terram (cf Gen 16:8), sacro velamine fidei tecti (cf
> Ex 29:6), accepturi coronas perveniunt (cf Rev 4:4).[10]

> [B]ene vale et ora pro nobis.[11]

---

[10]*PL*, vol. 106, cols. 52-53.

[11]Keefe, "An Unknown Response," p. 89, lines 37-38.

APPENDIX 1

THE EDITIONS OF THE CIRCULAR LETTER

INTERROGATIO CAROLI IMPERATORIS	KAROLI M. AD ODILBERTUM EPISTOLA	Caroli Magni epistola encyclica ad archiepiscopos de baptismo anni cir. 812.
IN NOMINE PATIS ET FILII, ET SPIRITUS SANCTI,	In nomine patris et filii et spiritus sancti.	In nomine patris et filii et spiritus sancti.
KAROLUS SERENISSIMUS AUGUSTUS A DEO CORONATUS, MAGNUS PACIFICUS IMPERATOR, ROMANUM GUBERNANS IMPERIUM, QUI ET PER MISERICORDIAM DEI REX FRANCORUM ET LANGOBARDORUM, AMALARIO VENERABILI EPISCOPO, AETERNAM IN DOMINO SALUTEM.	Karolus serenissimus augustus a deo coronatus, magnus pacificus imperator Romanum gubernans imperium, qui et per misericordiam dei rex Franchorum et Langobardorum, Odilberto venerabili archiepiscopo in domino salutem.	Karolus serenissimus augustus a deo coronatus, magnus pacificus imperator Romanum gubernans imperium, qui et per misericordiam dei rex Franchorum et Langobardorum, N. venerabili archiepiscopo in domino salutem.
1. Saepius tecum, immo et cum ceteris collegis tuis familiare conloquium de utilitate sanctae Dei ecclesiae habere voluissemus, si absque molestia corporali id efficere potuissetis.	Saepius tecum immo et cum ceteris collegis tuis familiare conloquium de utilitate sanctae dei ecclesiae habere voluissemus, si absque molestia corporali id effici potuisset	Saepius tecum immo et cum ceteris collegis tuis familiare conloquium de utilitate sanctae dei ecclesiae habere uoluissemus, si absque molestia corporali id effici potuisset.

2. Sed quamvis sanctitatem tuam in divinis rebus tota intentione vigilare non ignoremus, omittere tamen non possumus, quin tuam devotionem, Sancto incitante Spiritu nostris apicibus conpellamus atque commoneamus, ut magis ac magis in sancta Dei ecclesia studiose ac vigilanti cura laborare studeas in praedicatione sancta et doctrina salutari; quatenus per tuam devotissimam sollertiam verbum vitae aeternae crescat et currat, et multiplicetur numerus populi christiani in laudem et gloriam salvatoris nostri Dei.

3. Nosse itaque per tua scripta aut per te ipsum volumus qualiter tu et suffraganei tui doceatis et instruatis sacerdotes Dei et plebem vobis commissam de baptismi sacramento, id est cur primo infans catecuminus efficiatur, [1] vel quid sit catecuminus. [2]

4. Deinde per ordinem omnia quae aguntur.

Sed quamvis sanctitatem tuam in divinis rebus tota intentione vigilare non ignoremus, omittere tamen non possumus, quin tuam devotionem sancto incitante spiritu, nostris apicibus conpellamus atque commoneamus, ut magis ac magis in sancta dei ecclesia studiose ac vigilanti cura laborare studeas in praedicatione sancta et doctrina salutari, quatenus per tuam devotissimam sollertiam verbum vitae aeternae crescat et currat, et multiplicetur numerus populi christiani in laudem et gloriam salvatoris nostri dei.

Nosse itaque per tua scripta aut per te ipsum volumus qualiter tu et suffraganei tui doceatis et instruatis sacerdotes dei et plebem vobis commissam de baptismi sacramento, id est cur primo infans catecuminus efficiatur [1] vel quid sit catecuminus. [2]

Deinde per ordinem omnia quae aguntur.

Sed quamuis sanctitatem tuam in diuinis rebus tota intentione uigilare non ignoremus, omittere tamen non possumus, quin tuam deuotionem sancto incitante spiritu nostris conpellamus atque commoneamus apicibus, ut magis ac magis in sancta dei ecclesia studiose ac uigilanti cura laborare studeas in praedicatione sancta et doctrina salutari, quatenus per tuam deuotissimam sollertiam uerbum uitae aeternae crescat et currat, et multiplicetur numerus populi christiani in laudem et gloriam saluatoris nostri dei.

Nosse itaque per tua scripta aut per te ipsum uolumus qualiter tu et suffraganei tui doceatis et instruatis sacredotes dei et plebum uobis commissam de baptismi sacramento, id est cur primo infans catechumenus efficiatur [1] uel quid sit catechumenus. [2]

Deinde per ordinem omnia quae aguntur.

De scrutinio, quid sit scrutinium. [3]

De symbolo, quae sit eius interpretatio, secundum latinos. [4]

De credulitate, quomodo credendum sit in Deum Patrem omnipotentem, et in Iesum Christum Filium eius natum et passum, et in Spiritum Sanctum, sanctam ecclesiam catholicam, et cetera que secuntur in eodem symbolo. [5]

5. De abrenuntiatione satanae et de omnibus operibus eius atque pompis, quid sit abrenuntiatio, [6] vel quae opera diaboli et pompae, [7] cur exsuffletur [8] vel cur exorcizetur. [9]

Cur catecuminus accipiat salem, [10] quare tangantur nares, [11] pectus ungatur oleo. [12] Cur scapulae signantur,[13] quare pectus et scapulae liniantur. [14]

Cur albis induitur vestimentis? [15]

De scrutinio, quid sit scrutinium. [3]

De symbolo, quae sit eius interpretatio secundum Latinos. [4]

De credulitate, quomodo credendum sit in deum patrem omnipotentem, et in Iesum Christum filium eius, natum et passum, et in spiritum sanctum, sanctam ecclesiam catholicam et cetera quae sequuntur in eodem symbolo. [5]

De abrenuntiatione satanae et omnibus operibus eius atque pompis, quid sit abrenuntiatio, [6] vel quae opera diaboli et pompae eius. [7] Cur insufflatur [8] vel cur exorcizatur. [9]

Cur catechuminus accipit salem. [10] Quare tangantur nares [11], pectus ungatur oleo, [12] cur scapulae signantur. [13] Quare pectus et scapulae liniantur. [14]

Cur albis induitur vestimentis. [15]

De scrutinio, quid sit scrutinium. [3]

De symbolo, quae sit eius interpretatio secundum Latinos. [4]

De credulitate, quomodo credendum sit in deum patrem omnipotentem, et in Jesum Christum filium eius natum et passum, et in spiritum sanctum, sanctam ecclesiam catholicam et cetera quae sequuntur in eodem symbolo.[5]

De abrenuntiatione satanae et omnibus operibus eius atque pompis, quid sit abrenuntiatio, [6] uel quae opera diaboli et pompae eius. [7] Cur insufflatur [8] uel cur exorcizatur. [9]

Cur catechumenus accipit salem. [10] Quare tangantur nares [11], pectus ungatur oleo, [12] cur scapulae signantur. [13] Quare pectus et scapulae liniantur. [14]

Cur albis induitur uestimentis. [15]

6. Cur sacro chrismate caput perunguitur [16] et mystico tegitur velamine? [17]

Vel cur corpore et sanguine dominico confirmatur? [18]

Haec omnia subtili indagine per scripta nobis, sicut diximus, nuntiare satage, vel, si ita teneas et praedices, aut si in hoc quod praedicas, te ipsum custodias.

Bene vale et ora pro nobis.

Hannsens, pp. 235-236.

Cur sacro chrismate caput perungitur [16], et mystico tegitur velamine. [17]

Vel cur corpore et sanguine dominico confirmatur. [18]

Haec omnia subtili indagine per scripta nobis sicut diximus nuntiare satage, vel si ita teneas et praedices, aut si in hoc quod praedicas te ipsum custodias.

Bene vale et ora pro nobis.

Wiegand, pp. 23-25.

Cur sacro chrismate caput perungitur [16], et mystico tegitur uelamine. [17]

Vel cur corpore et sanguine dominico confirmatur. [18]

Haec omnia subtili indagine per scripta nobis sicut diximus nuntiare satage, uel si ita teneas et praedices, aut si in hoc quod praedicas te ipsum custodias.

Bene uale et ora pro nobis.

Heer, pp. 89-90.

APPENDIX 2

COMPARISON OF THE CIRCULAR LETTER WITH *PRIMO PAGANUS*

Excerpt from:

Excerpt from:

ALCUIN EPISTLE 134

KAROLI M. AD ODILBERTUM
EPISTOLA

Dümmler, *Epistolae karolini aevi,*
vol.2.

Wiegand, *Erzbischof Odilbert.*

Primo paganus caticumenus fit;
accedens ad baptismum, ut renuntiet
maligno spiritui et omnibus eius
damnosis pompis.

primo infans catechuminus efficitur [1]
vel quid sit catechuminus. [2]
Deinde per ordinem omnia quæ aguntur.

De scrutinio, quid sit scrutinium. [3]

Exsufflatur etiam, ut fugato diabolo
Christo deo nostro paretur introitus.

Exorcizatur, id est coniuratur malignus
spiritus ut exeat et recedat dans locum
Deo vero.

Accipit caticuminus salem, ut putrida et
fluxa eius peccata sapientiae sale divino
munere mundentur.

Diende symboli apostolici traditur ei
fides, ut vacua domus et a prisco
habitatore derelicta fide ornetur et
preparetur habitatio Dei.

De symbolo, quae sit eius interpretatio,
secundum Latinos. [4]

De credulitate, quomodo credendum sit
in deum patrem omnipotentem, et in
Iesum Christum filium eius natum et
passum, et in spiritum sanctum, sanctam
ecclesiam catholicam et cetera quæ
sequuntur in eodem symbolo. [5]

Tunc fiunt scrutinia, ut exploretur sepius
an post renuntiationem satanae sacra
verba datae fidei radicitus corde

defixerit.

De abrenuntiatione satanæ et de omnibus operibus eius atque pompis, quid sit abrenuntiatio, [6] vel quæ opera diaboli et pompæ eius. [7]

Cur insufflatur [8] vel cur exorcizatur. [9]

Cur catechuminus accipit salem. [10]

Tanguntur et nares, ut quamdiu spiritum naribus trahat, in fide accepta perduret.

Quare tangantur nares [11],

Pectus quoque eodem perunguiter oleo, ut signo sanctae crucis diabolo claudatur ingressus.

pectus ungatur oleo, [12]

Signantur et scapulae, ut undique muniatur.

cur scapulæ signantur. [13]

Item in pectoris et scapulae unctione signatur fidei firmitas et operum bonorum perseverantia.

Quare pectus et scapulæ liniantur. [14]

Et sic in nomine sanctae Trinitatis trina submersione baptizatur.

Et recte homo, qui ad imaginem sanctae Trinitatis conditus est, per invocationem sanctae Trinitatis ad eandem renovatur imaginem et qui tertio gradu peccati, id est consensu cecidit in mortem, tertio elevatus de fonte per gratiam resurgat ad vitam.

Tunc albis induitur vestimentis propter gaudium regenerationis et castitatem vitae et angelici splendoris decorem.

Cur albis induitur vestimentis. [15]

Tunc sacro chrismate caput perunguitur et mystico tegitur velamine, ut intellegat

Cur sacro chrismate caput perungitur [16], et mystico tegitur velamine. [17]

se diadema regni et sacerdotii dignitatem
portare iuxta apostolum : 'Vos estis
genus regale et sacerdotale, offerentes
vosmet Deo vivo hostiam sanctam et
Deo placentam'.[I Pet 2:9] Sic corpore
et sanguine dominico confirmatur, ut
illius sit capitis membrum, qui pro eo
passus est et resurrexit.

Vel cur corpore et sanguine dominico
confirmatur. [18]

Novissime per inpositionem manus a
summo sacerdote septiformis gratiae
spiritum accipit, ut roboretur per
Spiritum sanctum ad praedicandum aliis,
qui fuit in baptismo per gratiam vitae
donatus aeternae.

Appendix III

Manuscript and Edition Information

Keefe	Bouhot	Hanssens	Other

K01 - Response of Odilbert of Milan

St. Paul in Carinthia, SB	*Saint-Paul-en-Carinthie*, Archiv des Benediktinerstiftes		
5/1, s. IX 2/3 Reichenau	25.2-35(xxv.a.5) xe s.		
		St Gall 40	

Edition:
a) F. Wiegand, *Erzbischof Odilbert*, pp. 27-37.
b) J. Mabillon, *Veterum Analectorum*, vol. 4, pp. 317-322 (second ed. pp. 76-77).
c) P. Jaffé, ed., *Monumenta Carolina*, pp. 403-406.
b and c give an edition of the letter of Odilbert and the titles of the chapters of the florilegium, but not the text.

K05 - Anonymous

St. Paul in Carinthia, SB 5/1, s. IX 2/3 Reichenau			
Bamberg Staatl. Bibl. Lit. 131 s. IX 4/4 or IX/X S. Ger			
Mantua Bibl. Com. 331, s. XI Polirone			

174

Paris
BN
lat. 2389,
s. XI/XII

Vatican
Bibl. Apost.
Vat. lat. 1147
(further copies:
Vat. lat. 1146;
1148;*Vienna,*
ÖNB lat. 914)
s. XI

Munich
Bayer. Staatsbibl.
Clm 5127
s. XI & XII

Munich
Bayer. Staatsbibl.
Clm 14581
s. XI/XII
Regensburg

Edition: none

K10 - Anonymous
Autun
Bibl. mun.
184 (G. III)
s. IX 2/3
W. Fr. (not Tours)
(fragment - incipit)

Vatican
Bibl. Apost. Vat.
Reg. lat. 69
s. IX 2/2, Tours?

Paris
BN
lat. 5577, s. XI

Edition:
A. Wilmart, *Analecta reginensis*, pp. 166-170.

K12 - Anonymous

Paris	*Paris*
BN	B.N.
lat. 1248, s. XI ½	lat. 1248 xe s.
	St. Martial de
Limoges	Limoges

Monte Cassino
Arch. dell'Abb.
323 s. IX 2/2
cent. It.

Eichstätt
Bischöfl.
Ordinariatsarch.1
1071-3
with additions

Bamberg
Staatl. Bibl.
Lit. 53, s. XI
Bamberg

Bamberg
Staatl. Bibl.
Lit. 133, s. XI

London
BL
Add. 17004, s. XI
Ger.

Monte Cassino
Arch. dell'Abb.
451, s. XI
Monte Cassino

176

Munich Bayer. Staatsbibl. Clm 6425, s. XI Freising	Munich Staatsbibliothek 6425		
Vienna ÖNB lat. 701, s. XI Mainz			
Wolfenbüttel Herz-Aug. Bibl. Helmst. 493 [530] s. XII in. Anspach?			
Wolfenbiittel Herz.-Aug. Bibl. Helmst. 141 [164] s. XII ½ Ger.			
Vienna ÖNB lat. 1817 s. XII 2/2	*Vienne* Nationalbibliothek 1817 xiie s.		
Bamberg Staatl. Bibl. Lit. 140, s. XII			
Fiecht SB 113, s. XII			
Heiligenkreuz SB 153, s. XII			
Lambach SB XXVII, s. XII			

177

St. Florian
SB
466, s. XII

Tours
Bibl. mun. 136
s. XIII

Editions:
a) M. Gerbert, *Monumenta veteris liturgiae Alemannicae*, vol. 2. St. Blasien: St. Blaise Press, 1779, pp. 210-211.
b) C. Vogel, R. Elze, *Le Pontifical*, vol. 2, pp. 172-176.

K14 - version to Amalar of Trier

Zürich	*Zurich*	*Zurich*	Jaffé, *Monumenta*
Zentralbibl.	Zentralbibliothek		
Car. C. 102,	Car. C.102 (268)	C. 102	Cod. C102
s. IX 3/3,	ixe-xe s.		saec. x
Switz.-N. It.			
Arras	Arras		
Bibl. mun.	*Bibl.* Mun.		
685, s. XII	685 (741), xiie s		

Editions:
a) F. Forster, ed., *Beati Flacci Albini sev Alcvini Abbatis, Caroli Magni regis ac imperatoris, magistri: Opera*. New and expanded edition, vol. 2. Regensburg: S. Emmerami, 1777, p. 520.
b) P. Jaffé, ed., *Monumenta Carolina*, pp. 402-403.
c) *PL*, vol. 99, col. 892.
d) Societas Aperiendis Fontibus Rerum Germanicarum Medii Aevi, ed., *Epistolae karolini aevi* vol. 3, p. 242.
e) J.M. Hanssens, *Amalarii*, vol. 1, pp. 235-236.
f) S.A. Keefe, "An Unknown Response," *RB* 96 (1986): 87-89.

K14 - version to Odilbert of Milan

St. Paul in Carinthia, SB	*Saint-Paul-en-Carinthie*, Archiv des Benediktinerstiftes	*St Paul de Carinthie*	Jaffé, *Monumenta St. Paul in Carinthia*
5/1,	25.2-35 (xxv.a.5)		cod. xxv
s. IX 2/3,	xe s.	xxv a/5	s. x
Reichenau			

178

Paris	Paris		
BN	B.N,		
lat. 2389	lat. 2389		
s. XI or XII	xie s.		

Editions:

a) J. Mabillon, ed., *Veterum analectorum*, vol. 1, p. 21, (second ed., pp. 75-76).

b) J. Baluz, *Capitularia Regum Francorum (Additae sunt Marculfi Monachi & aliorum Formulae veteres et Notae doctissimorum Virorum)*, 2 vols. Paris: F. Muguet, 1677 (2nd ed. Paris: Quillau/ Morin, 1780), vol. 1, cols 483/484.

c) P. Jaffé, ed., *Monumenta Carolina*, pp. 401-402.

d) J. Mansi, *Sacrorum Conciliorum*, vol. 17/2, col. 483/484.

e) *PL*, vol. 98, cols. 933-934.

f) F. Wiegand, *Erzbischof Odilbert*, pp. 25-27.

K14 - version to 'N.'

Vienna	Vienne		
ÖNB	Nationalbibliothek		
lat. 398, s. XII	398, xiie s.		

Zwettl	Zwettl		
SB	Stiftsbibliothek		
283, s. XIII	283		

Edition:

J.M. Heer, *Ein karolingischer Missions-Katechismus*, pp. 89-90.

K15 - Magnus of Sens

Angers	Angers		
Bibl. mun.	Bibl. Mun.		
277, s. IX 3/4	277 (268) ixe s. fin		
	Saint Aubin		
Angers?			

Paris	Paris		
BN	B.N.		
lat. 10741, s. IX	lat.10741 ixe-xe s.		
3/3, area of Lyon			

Paris	Paris		
BN	B.N.		
lat. 13655	lat. 13656		
s. X 1/2 or med.	début du xie s.		

Paris BN nouv. acq. lat. 450, s. X	*Paris* B.N. Nouv. Acq. lat . 450 ixe-xe s.		
Only 13655 has the preface and original incipit/explicit	Also a manuscript of Corbie (citing J. Sirmond)		
			Martene: Ex Ms Coisliniano
			Keefe, "An Uknown response," adds *Florence* Bibl. Med. Laur. S. Marco 669, s. xiii

Editions:

a) E. Martene, *De Antiquis Ecclesiae ritibus libri quator collecti ex variis insigniorum Ecclesiarum Pontificalibus, Sacramentariis, Missalibus, Breviariis, Ritualibus, libris seu Manualibus, Ordinariis seu Consuetudinariis, cum manuscriptis tum editis; ex diversis Conciliorum Decretis, Episcoporum Statutis aliisque probatis auctoribus permultis.*, 2nd ed. Antwerp: J.B. de la Bry, 1736-1738, vol. 1, cols. 169-171. 1st edition 3 vols. (Rouen: G. Behourt, 1700-1703), vol. 1, pp.158-161.

b) *PL*, vol. 102, cols. 981-984.

c) S.A. Keefe, "An Unknown Response," *RB* 96 (1986): 56-60.

K23 - Amalarius of Trier

Vatican Bibl. Apost. Vat. Reg. lat. 284 s. IX 2/3 N. half of Fr. (not Fleury)	*Vatican* Biblioteca Apostolica, Reg. lat. 284, ixe s.		
Freiburg i. Br. Universitätsbibl. 8, s. IX 2/2, E. Fr.			

Paris BN lat. 10741, s. IX 3/3 area of Lyon		
St. Gall SB 446 s. IX 3/3, St. Gall	*Saint-Gall* Stiftsbibliothek 446 xe s.	
Zürich Zentralbibl. Car. C. 102 s. IX 3/3 Switz.- N. It.	*Zurich* Zentralbibliothek Car. C. 102 (268) ixe-xe s.	Jaffé: *Zurich* Cod C102
Angers Bibl. mun. 277, s. IX 3/4 Angers?	*Angers* Bibl. Mun. 277 (268) fin du ixe s.	
Munich Bayer. Staatsbibl. Clm 13581 s. IX, W. Fr. mostly	*Munich* Staatsbibliothek 13581 fin du ixe s.	
St. Paul in *Carinthia* SB 10/1, s. X	Saint-Paul-en- Carinthie, *Archiv* *des* *Benediktinerstiftes* 25.2.20	manuscrit autrefois à S.Blaise, aujourd'hui à *St-Paul de-* *Carinthie* 25/2/20
Paris BN nouv. acq. lat. 450 s. X	*Paris* B.N., nouv. acq. lat. 450 ixe-xe s.	*Paris* Nouv. Acq. lat. 450 (IXe,-Xe s.)

Einsiedeln SB 110, s. XI in.	*Einsiedeln* Stiftsbibliothek 110, xie s.	
Stuttgart Würt. Landesbibl. HB. VI. 108 s. XI 2/2 S.W.. Ger.	*Stuttgart* Landesbibliothek HB. l08 xie s.	
Arras Bibl. mun. 685, s. XII	*Arras* Bibl. Mun. 685 (741), xiie s.	*Arras* 685 (XIIe s.)

Editions:

a) H. Canisius, ed., *Antiquae Lectiones, seu antiqva monvmenta ad historiam mediae aetatis illvstrandam*. Ingolstadt: A. Angermarium, 1604, vol. 6, pp. 369-379.

b) A. Quercetanus [Duchesne], *B. Flacci Albini*, cols. 1151-1122.

c) C. Lacointe, *Annales ecclesiastici francorum ab Anno Christi 417 ad annum 845*, 8 vols. Paris: 1665-1683, vol. 7, pp. 209ff.

d) J. Basnage, *Thesaurus monumentorum ecclesiasticorum et historicorum, sive Henrici Canisii lectiones antiquae ad saeculorum ordinem digestae variisque opusculis auctae, quibus praefationes historicas, animadversiones criticas, et notas in singulos auctores, ajecit Jacobus Basnage, cum indicibus locupletissimis*, 4 vols. Amsterdam: R. & G. Wetstenios, 1725, vol. 2/1, pp. 543-548.

e) J.N. von Hontheim, *Historia Trevirensis diplomatica et pragmatica, inde a translata Treveri Praefectura Praetorio Falliarum ad haec usque tempora*, 3 vols. Augsburg and Wurzburg: M. Veith, 1750, vol. 1, pp. 158-163.

f) F. Forster, *Alcuini opera*, vol. 2, pp. 520-524.

g) M. Gerbert, ed., *Monumenta veteris liturgiae alemannicae*, vol. 2, pp. 264-269.

h) P. Jaffé, ed., *Monumenta Carolina*, pp. 406-409 (only the protocol and eschatacol to the letter, not the part concerning the rites).

i) *PL*, vol. 99, cols. 893-902.

j) Societas aperiendis fontibus rerum germanicarum medii aevi, ed., *Epistolae karolini aevi*, vol. 3, pp. 242-244 (also excluding the section on the baptismal rites).

k) Hanssens, *Amalarii*, vol. 1, pp. 236-251.

K25 Liedrad of Lyons

| *Paris* BN lat. 12262 s. IX ca. med., Fr. | *Paris* B.N., lat 12262 ixe s. Saint-Éloi de Noyon | | Dümmler: *Paris* 12262 S. Germani 794 x |

| *Paris* BN lat. 1008 s. IX & X, Fr. | *Paris* B.N. lat. 1008 ixe s. | | Dümmler: *Paris* P 1008 IX |

| *Barcelona* Bibl. Univ. 228 s. X 2/2- XI S.E..Fr. or N. It. | *Barcelone* Biblioteca Universitaria 228(20.5.16) xe-xie s. | | |

Unidentified
(Mabillon)
Villeneuve lès-Avignon
St. André-lez-Avignon

Editions:
a) J. Mabillon, *Veterum analectorum*, vol. 3: pp. 1-28 (second ed. pp. 78-85).
b) P. Jaffé, ed., *Monumenta Carolina*, pp. 410-411 (only the protocol and eschatacol, not the section concerning the rites).
c) E. Dümmler, *Epistolae Karolini aevi*, vol. 2, pp. 539-540 (also excluding the section on the rites).
d) *PL*, vol. 99, cols. 853-872 (a copy of edition 'a').

K30 - Jessie of Amiens
Florence
Bibl. Med.
Laurenz. Aedil.
214, s. XII/XIII

St. Gall	Saint-Gall		
SB	Stiftsbibliothek		
124, ca. 804-820	124, ixe s.		
area of St. Amand			
(N.E. Fr.)			
Vatican	Vatican		
Bibl. Apost. Vat.	Biblioteca		
Pal. lat. 485	Apostolica		
s. IX ca. med.	Pal. lat. 485		
	deuxième moitié		
	du ixe s. (avant		
	875) abbaye de		
Lorsch	Lorsch		
Paris	Paris		
BN	B.N.		
lat. 13372	lat 13372		
s. XII	xiie s.		
	abbaye du Mont-		
	Saint-Éloy		
unidentified	unidentified		

Editions:

a) J. Cordes, ed., *Opuscula et epistolae Hincmari Remensis archiepiscopi accesserunt Nicolai PP. I et aliorum eiusdem aevi quaedam epistolae et scripta*, Paris: Cramoisy, 1615, pp. 664-685.

b) *PL*, vol 105, cols. 781-791.

K33 - Maxentius of Aquileia

Munich	Munich		Dümmler
Bayer. Staatsbibl.	Staatsbibliothek		Cod. Monac.
Clm 14410	14410		14410
			(S. Emmerammi
	premier tiers		E XXXIII)
s. IX 1/3	du ixe s.		ix
N. It. or Bavaria			

Editions:

a) B. Pez, ed., *Thesaurus anecdotorum*, vol. 2, cols. 8-12.

b) *PL*, vol. 106, cols. 51-54 (a copy of edition 'a').

c) E. Dümmler, *Epistolae karolini aevi*, vol. 2, pp. 537-539.

184

d) J.M. Heer, *Ein karolingischer Missions-Katechismus*, pp. 90-95.

K34 - Arno of Salzburg?

		Bouhot: "Alcuin,"
Vienna		*Vienne*
ÖNB		
lat. 1370		1370
s. IX 1-2/4,		
Mondsee		

Edition: None.

K38 - Anonymous

Munich		
Bayer. Staatsbibl.		
Clm 14410		
s. IX 1/3		
N. It. or Bavaria		

Editions:
a) B. Pez, *Thesaurus anecdotorom*, vol. 2/2, cols. 12-16.
b) *PL*, vol. 106, cols. 56-58.
c) J.M. Heer, *Ein karolingischer Missions-Katechismus*, pp. 97-101.

K41 - Hildebald of Cologne?

			Hanssens, *Amalarii:*
Wolfenbüttel	*Wolfenbüttel*		*Wolfenbüttel*
Herz.-	Herzog -		Herzog-
Aug. Bibl.	Augustbibliothek		Augustbibliothek c. lat. 4159
Weissenb. 75 [4159]	Weiss. 75 (4159)		(Wissenburgensis 75)
s. X 2/2 - XI/XII	xie-xiie s.		
Munich	*Munich*	*Munich*	*München*
Bayer.			Bayerische
Staatsbibl.	Staatsbibliotliek		Staatsbibliothek
Clm 21568	21568	21 568	c. lat. 21568
s. XII	xiie s.		

Incomplete:

Brussels Bibl. Roy. 6828-6869 s. XVII	*Bruxelles,* Bibliothèque Royale 6828-6869 (4495) xviie s.	*Bruxelles* Bibliothèque Royale 6828-6869

Brussels Bibl. Roy. 17349-17360 s. XVIII	*Bruxelles* Bibl.Royale 17349-17360 (6699), xviiie s.	*Bruxelles* 17349-17360

Editions:
a) J.M. Hanssens, "Deux documents carolingiens sur le bapteme," *EL* 41 (1927): 79-80. b) G. Morin, "Note sur un lettre attribuée faussement a Amalaire de Trèves dans le manuscrit lat 21568 de Munich," *RB* 13 (1896): 290-291.
c) Hanssens, *Amalarii*, vol. 3, pp. 269-271.

K42 - Anonymous

Vatican Bibl. Apost. Vat. Pal. lat. 485 s. IX ca. med. Lorsch	*Vatican* Biblioteca Apostolica Pal. Lat. 485 ixe s. 2/2

Edition:
C. De Clerq, "Ordines unctionis infirmi IXe et Xe siècle," *EL* 44 (1930): 120-122.

K50 Anonymous

Barcelona Bibl. Univ. 228, s. X 2/2-XI S.E.. Fr. or N. It.	*Barcelone* Biblioteca Universitaria 228 xe-xie s.

Vercelli Bibl. Capit. CXLIII, s. X 2/2 very prob. N. It.	*Verceil* Archivo Capitolare Eusebiana CXLIII ixe s. (xie s. additions)

186

El Escorial
Real Bibl. de S.
Lor. Q. III. 10, s.
XII ex.

Editions:
a) A. Wilmart (ed.)(posth.), "Une catéchèse baptismale du IXe siècle." *RB* 57
(1947): 196-200, using manuscript 'a' only.
b) J.M. Casas Homs, 'Dos antiguos tratados catequisticos,' *Spanische
Forschungen der Gorresgellschaft*, Erste Reihe Band 16-1. (1960): 77-84.

K51 - Anonymous
Paris
BN
lat. 1012, s. IX 1/3

Edition: None

K53 - Anonymous
Unidentified Manuscript
Editions:
a) E. Martène and U. Durand, *Thesaurus novus anecdotorum*, 5 vols. 2nd ed.,
Paris: F. Delaulne, H. Foucault, M. Clouzier, J.G. Nyon, S. Ganeau & N.
Gosselin, 1717, vol. 1: *Complectens regum ac principum aliorumque virorum
illustrium epistolas et diplomata bene multa*, col. 15-17.
b) *PL*, vol. 98, cols. 938-939 (copy of edition 'a').
c) E. Dümmler, *Karolini epistolae aevi*, vol. 2, pp. 535-37 (copy of edition 'a').

K55 - Anonymous
Vienna
ÖNB
lat. 823, s. IX 2/2
W. Ger. or E. Fr.

Paris
BN
lat 13092, s. XI

Edition: None.

BIBLIOGRAPHY

1. Texts and Commentary.

Andrieu, M. *Les ordines romani du haut moyen âge*. 5 vols. Vol. 1: *Les manuscrits*, vols. 2-5: *Les textes*. Spicilegium Sacrum Lovaniense: Études et documents, vols. 11, 23, 24, 28, 29. Louvain, Spicilegium Sacrum Lovaniense, 1931-1961.

--------. "Le sacre épiscopal d'après Hincmar de Reims." *Revue d'histoire ecclesiastique*, 58 (1962): 22-73.

Baluz, S. *Capitularia Regum Francorum (Additae sunt Marculfi Monachi & aliorum Formulae veteres et Notae doctissimorum Virorum)*. 2 vols. Paris, F. Muguet, 1677 (2nd ed., Paris, Quillau/ Morin, 1780).

Basnage, J. *Thesaurus monumentorum ecclesiasticorum et historicorum, sive Henrici Canisii lectiones antiquae ad saeculorum ordinem digestae variisque opusculis auctae, quibus praefationes historicas, animadversiones criticas, et notas in singulos auctores, adjecit Jacobus Basnage, cum indicibus locupletissimis,* 4 vols. Amsterdam: R. & G. Wetstenios, 1725, vol. 2/1, pp. 543-548.

Bischoff, B. *Die südostdeutschen Schreibschulen und Bibliotheken in der Karolingerzeitz*. 2 vols., 2nd edn. Weisbaden, Harrassowitz, 1960 and 1980.

Boretius, A., ed. *Capitvlaria Regvm Francorvm*, vol. 1. MGH, Legum, Section 2, vol. 1. Hanover, Hahn, 1883.

Bouhot, J.-P. "Explications du rituel baptismal à l'époque carolingienne." *Revue des études augustiniennes* 24 (1978): 278-301.

--------. "Alcuin et le 'De catechizandis rudibus' de saint Augustin." *Recherches augustiniennes* 15 (1980): 205-230.

Burn, "Neue Texte zur Geschichte des apostolischen Symbols." Zeitschrift für Kirchengeschichte 25 (1904): 148-154.

188

Canisius, H., ed., *Antiqvae lectiones, sev antiqva monvmenta ad historiam mediae aetatis illvstrandam.* 6 vols. Ingolstadt, A. Angermarium, 1601-1604.

Cappelle, B. "L'origine antiadoptianiste de notre texte du Symbole de la Messe." *Recherches de théologie ancienne et médievale,* 1(1929): 7-20.

Carpenter, H.J. "*Symbolum* as a Title of the Creed." *Journal of Theological Studies,* first series, 43 (1942): 1-11.

Casas Homs, J.M. "Dos antiguos tratados catequisticos." *Spanische Forschungen der Görresgesellschaft,* Erste Reihe, vol. 16-1 (1960): 77-84.

Chavasse, A., ed. "Sermo In nativitate domini (1)." *Sancti Leonis magni romani pontificis tractatvs septem et nonaginta.* CCL, vol. 138. Turnhout, Brepols, 1973, pp. 88-89.

Cordes, J., ed. *Opuscula et epistolae Hincmari Remensis archiepiscopi accesserunt Nicolai PP. I et aliorum eiusdem aevi quaedam epistolae et scripta.* Paris, Cramoisy, 1615.

Dahlhaus-Berg, E. *Nova antiquitas et antiqua novitas Typologische Exegese und isidorianisches Geschichtsbild bei Theodulf von Orléans.* Kölner historische Abhandlungen, vol. 23. Vienna-Cologne, Böhlau, 1975.

De Clercq, C. *La législation religeuse franque de Clovis à Charlemagne (507-814).* Recueil de travaux publiés par les membres des Conférences d'Histoire et de Philologie, series 2, vol. 38. Paris, Bureaux du Recueil Bibliothèque de l'Université and Louvain, Librarie du Recueil Sirey, S.A., 1936.

--------, "Ordines unctionis infirmi IXe et Xe siècle." *EL* 44 (1930): 120-122.

DeRubeis, B.M. *Dissertationes duae: prima pe Turrianio, seu Tyrannio Rufino monacho & presbytero: altera de vetustis liturgicis aliisque sacris Ritibus, qui vigebant olim in aliquibus Forojuliensis provinciæ ecclesiis.* Venice, S. Occhi, 1754.

Deshusses, J., ed. *Le sacramentaire grégorien: Ses principales formes d'après les plus anciens manuscrits.* Vol. 1, *Le Sacramentaire, le supplément d'Aniane,* comparative ed., 2nd ed., revised and corrected. Spicilegium Friburgense, vol. 16. Fribourg, Editions Fribourg Suisse, 1979.

Quercetanus [Du Chesne], A., ed. B. *Flacci Albini sive Alchuuini, Abbatis, Karoli Magni regis, ac imperatoris, Magistri: Opera quae hactenus reperiri potuerunt: Nonnulla auctius et emendatius; pleraque nunc primum ex codd. mss. edita. Accessere B. Paulini Aquileiensis Patriarchae Contra Felicem Vrgel. episc.* Paris, S. Cramoisy, 1617.

Dümmler, E., ed. *Epistolae karolini aevi.* Vol. 2. MGH, Epistolae, vol. 4. Berlin, Weidmann, 1895.

--------. *Poetae Latini aevi Carolini.* Vol. 1. MGH, Poetarvm Latinorvm medii aevi, vol. 1. Berlin, Weidmann, 1881.

Dumas, A., ed. *Liber Sacramentorum Gellonensis.* CCL, vol. 159. Turnhout, Brepols, 1981.

Étaix, R. "Un manuel pastorale de l'époche carolingienne." *RB* 91 (1981): 115-123.

Forster, F., ed. *Beati Flacci Albini sev Alcvini Abbatis, Caroli Magni regis ac imperatoris, magistri: Opera.* New and expanded edition, vol. 2. Regensburg, S. Emmerami, 1777.

Franz, A. *Die Messe im deutschen Mittelalter: Beträge zur Geschichte der Liturgie und des religiösen Volkslebens.* 1st ed., Freiburg im Breisgau, Herder, 1902. Reprint ed., Darmstadt, Wissenschaftliche Buschgesellschaft, 1963.

Freeman, A. "Theodulf of Orleans and the *Libri Carolini*." *Speculum* 32 (1957): 663-705.

Fuhrmann, H., ed. *Das Constitutum Constantini (Konstantinische Schenkung): Text.* MGH, Fontes Iuris Germanici Antiqui, in usum scholarum, vol. 10. Hanover, Hahn, 1968.

Gerbert, M. *Monumenta veteris liturgiae Alemannicae.* 2 vols. St. Blasien, St. Blaise Press, 1777-1779.

Hänggi, A., Schönherr, A., eds. *Sacramentarium Rhenaugiense.* Spicilegium Friburgense, vol. 15. Freibourg, Switzerland, Universitätsverlag, 1970.

Hanssens, J.M. *Amalarii episcopi opera liturgica omnia.* Vol. 1. StT, vol. 138. Vatican City, Polyglott Press, 1948.

190

--------, "Deux documents carolingiens sur le bapteme." *EL* 41 (1927): 69-82.

Heer, J.M. *Ein karolingischer Missions-Katechismus: Ratio de cathecizandis rudibus und die Tauf-Katechesen des Maxentius von Aquileia und eines Anonymus im Kodex Emmeram. XXXIII saec. IX.* Biblische und Patristische Forschungen, vol. 1. Freiburg im Breisgau, Herder, 1911.

Jaffé, P., ed. *Monumenta Carolina.* Bibliotheca rerum germanicarum, vol. 4. Berlin, Weidmann, 1867.

Keefe, S.A. "An Unknown Response From the Archiepiscopal Province of Sens to Charlemagne's Circulatory Inquiry on Baptism." *RB* 96 (1986): 48-93.

--------. "Carolingian Baptismal Expositions: A Handlist of Tracts and Manuscripts." Blumenthal, U.-R. ed. *Carolingian Essays: Andrew W. Mellon Lectures in Early Christian Studies.* Washington, D.C., The Catholic University of America Press, 1983: pp. 169-273.

--------. "The Claim of Authorship in Carolingian Baptismal Expositions: The Case of Odilbert of Milan." *Fälschungen im Mittelalter: Internationaler Kongreß der Monumenta Germaniae Historica, München, 16.-19. September 1986.* MGH, Schriften, vol. 33/5, *Fingierte Briefe Frömmigkeit und Fälschung Realienfälschungen.* Hanover, Hahn, 1988), pp. 385-401.

--------. *Water and the Word: Baptism and the Education of the Clergy in the Carolingian Empire: A Study of Texts and Manuscripts.* University of Notre Dame Press, forthcoming, 1998.

Lacointe, C. *Annales ecclesiastici francorum ab Anno Christi 417 ad annum 845.* 8 vols.. Paris: 1665-1683.

Lawson, C., ed. *Sancti Isidori episcopi Hispalensis, De ecclesiasticis officiis.* CCL, vol.113. Turnhout, Brepols, 1989.

Lindsay, W.M., ed. *Isidori Hispalensis Episcopi etymologiarvm sive originvm, libri XX.* 2 vols. Oxford, Clarendon Press, 1911.

Lowe, E.A., ed. *The Bobbio Missal: A Gallican Mass-Book (MS. Paris Lat. 13246).* The Henry Bradshaw Society, vol. 58. London, Harrison & Sons, 1920.

McKitterick, R. *The Frankish Church and the Carolingian Reforms 789-895.* Royal Historical Society Studies in History, vol. 2. London, Royal Historical Society, 1977.

Mabillon, J. *De liturgia Gallicana, libri III.* Paris, E. Martin and J. Boudot, 1685.

--------. *Veterum analectorum complectens varia fragmenta & epistolia scriptorum ecclesiasticorum, tam prosa, quam metro, hactenus inedita.* 4 vols. Paris, L. Billaine/E. Martin & J. Boudot, 1675-1685. 2nd ed. published in one volume as *Vetera analecta.* Paris, Montalant, 1723.

Mansi, J., ed. *Sacrorum Conciliorum nova et amplissima collectio.* 53 vols. Florence/Venice: 1759-1798, facsimilie reproduction. Arnheim/Paris/Leipzig, H. Welter, 1901-1927.

Martene, E. *De Antiquis Ecclesiae ritibus libri quator collecti ex variis insigniorum Ecclesiarum Pontificalibus, Sacramentariis, Missalibus, Breviariis, Ritualibus, libris seu Manualibus, Ordinariis seu Consuetudinariis, cum manuscriptis tum editis; ex diversis Conciliorum Decretis, Episcoporum Statutis aliisque probatis auctoribus permultis.* 2nd ed., 4 vols. Antwerp, J.B. de la Bry, 1736-1738. 1st ed., 3 vols. Rouen, G. Behourt, 1700-1703

Martene, E., Durand, U. *Thesaurus novus anecdotorum.* 5 vols. 2nd ed. Paris, F. Delaulne, H. Foucault, M. Clouzier, J.G. Nyon, S. Ganeau & N. Gosselin, 1717.

Mohlberg, L.C. ed. *Missale Gothicum (Vat. Reg. Lat. 317).* Rerum Ecclesiasticarum Documenta, Series Maior, Fontes, vol. 5. Rome, Herder, 1961.

Mohlberg, L.C., Eizenhöfer, L., Siffrin, P. *Liber sacramentorum romanae aeclesiae ordinis anni circuli (Cod. Vat. Reg. lat. 316/Paris Bibl. Nat. 7193, 41/56) (Sacramentarium Gelasianum).* Rerum Ecclesiasticarum Documenta, Series Maior, Fontes, vol. 4. 3rd ed. Rome, Herder, 1981.

Morin, G. "Note sur un lettre attribuée faussement à Amalaire de Trèves dans le manuscrit lat. 21568 de Munich." *RB* 13 (1896): 289-294.

--------. "Texts inédits relatif au symbôle et la vie chrétienne." *RB* 22 (1905): 513-514.

192

Mühlbacher, E., ed. *Die Urkunden Pippins, Karlmanns und Karls des Grossen.* MGH, Diplomata Karolinorvm, vol. 1. Hanover, Hahn, 1906.

Pertz, G.H., Kurze, F., eds. *Annales fuldenses sive Annales regni Francorum orientalis ab Einhardo, Ruodolfo, Meginhardo fuldensibus, Seligenstadi, Fuldae, Mogontiaci consripti cum continuationibus ratisbonensi et altahensibus.* MGH, Scriptores rerum Germanicarum in usum scholarum separatim editi, vol. 7. Hanover, Hahn, 1891.

--------. *Annales regni Francorum inde ab a. 741 usque ad a. 829 qui dicuntur Annales laurissenses maiores et Einhardi.* MGH, Scriptores rerum Germanicarum in usum scholarum separatim editi, vol. 6. Hanover, Hahn, 1895.

Pez, B., ed. *Thesaurus anecdotorum, nouissimus seu Veterum Monumentorum praecipue Ecclesiasticorum, ex Germanicis potissimum Bibliothecis adornata Collectio recentissima.* 6 vols. Augsburg, P., M., & J. Veith, 1721-1728.

Pokorny, R. "Zur Taufumfrage Karls des Grossen." *ALW* 26 (1984): 166-173.

Porter, H.B. "Maxentius of Aquileia and the North Italian Baptismal Rites." *EL* 69 (1955): 3-9.

Romagnoli, H., ed. *Vitruvii, De architectura libri.* 2 vols. Romanorum Scriptorum Corpus Italicarum. Milan, S.A. Notari, 1933.

Saint-Roche, P., ed. *Liber Sacramentorum Engolismensis.* CCL, vol. 169C. Turnhout: Brepols, 1987.

Societas Aperiendis Fontibus Rerum Germanicarum Medii Aevi, eds. *Epistolae Merowingici et Karolini aevi.* Vol. 1. MGH, Epistolarum, vol. 3. Berlin, Weidmann, 1892.

Vogel, C., Elze, R., eds. *Le pontifical romano-germanique du Xe siècle. Le Texte.* Vol. 2. StT 227. Vatican City, Polyglott, 1963.

Von Hontheim, J.N. *Historia Trevirensis diplomatica et pragmatica, inde a translata Treveri Praefectura Praetorio Falliarum ad haec usque tempora.* 3 vols. Augsburg and Wurzburg, M. Veith, 1750.

--------. *Prodromus Historiæ Trevirensis Diplomaticæ et Pragmaticæ in duas partes Tributus.* 2 vols. Augsburg, I. & F. Veith, 1757.

Waitz, G., ed. *Einhard: Vita Karoli magni.* 6th ed. MGH, Scriptores rerum Germanicarum in usum scholarum separatim editi, vol. 25. Hanover, Hahn, 1911.

Warner, G.F. *The Stowe Missal.* The Henry Bradshaw Soceity, vol. 32. London, Harrison & Sons, 1915.

Werminghoff, A., ed. *Concilia aevi karolini.* Vol. 1. MGH, Legum, Section 3: Concilia, vol. 2/1. Hanover, Hahn, 1979.

Wiegand, F. *Erzbischof Odilbert von Mailand über die Taufe: Ein Beitrag zur Geschichte der Taufliturgie im Zeitalter Karls des Großen.* Studien zur Geschichte der Theologie und der Kirche, Bonwetsch, N., Seeberg, R., eds., vol. 4/1. Leipzig, 1899. Reprint ed., Aalen, Scientia Verlag, 1972.

Wilmart, A., ed. *Analecta reginensia, Extraits des manuscrits Latins de la reine Christine conservés au Vatican,* StT, vol. 59. Vatican City, Polyglott Press, 1933.

--------., (ed.)(posth.), "Une catéchèse baptismale du IXe siècle." *RB* 57 (1947): 196-200.

2. Pre-ninth and Ninth Century Baptismal Practice.

AA.VV., *Culto cristiano e politica imperiale carolingio.* Todi, Academia Tudertina, 1979.

Angenendt, A. "Die Taufe im frühen Mittelalter." AA.VV., *Segni e riti nella chiesa alto-medievale occidentale.* Spoleto, Centro Italiano di Studi sull'Alto Medioevo, 1987: 11-17.

--------, "Taufe und Politik im fruhen Mittelalter." *Frühmittelalter Studien* 7 (1973): 143-168.

Banting, J.M.H. "The Imposition of Hands in Confirmation: A Medieval Problem." *Journal of Theological Studies* 57 (1956): 147-159.

Beatrice P.F. *La lavanda dei piedi: contributo alla storia delle antiche liturgie Cristiane.* Bibliotheca 'Ephemerides Liturgicae,' 'Subsidia,' vol. 28. Rome, Centro liturgico Vincenziano, Edizione Liturgiche, 1983.

Beck, H. *The Pastoral Care of Souls in Southeast France During the Sixth Century.* Analecta Greagoriana, vol. 51, series facultatis hist. Ecclesiasticae, Section b, vol. 8. Rome, Pontificia Universitas Gregoriana, 1950.

Borella, P. "La confermazione all'epoca carolingia." *La confirmation.* Turin, Elle Di Ci, 1967.

Bragança, J.O. "Le symbolisme des rites baptismaux au moyen âge." *Didaskalia* 3 (1973): 37-56.

Chavasse, A. "La carême romain et les scrutins prébaptismaux avant le ixe siècle." *Recherches de science religiuese* 35 (1938): 325-381.

Cruz, A.E. "Le rôle du *De catechizandis rudibus* de Saint Augustin dans la catéchèse missionnaire dés 710 jusqu'à 847." *Studia Patristica*, vol. 11, Texte und Untersuchungen, vol. 108. Berlin, Akademie, 1972, pp. 316-321.

De Puniet, P. "La liturgie baptismal en Gaul avant Charlemagne." *Revue des questions historiques* 72 (1902): 283-423.

Dondeyne, A. "La discipline des scrutins dans l'Église latine avant Charlemagne." *Revue d'histoire ecclésiastiques* 52 (1932): 5-33, 751-787.

Duchesne, L. *Origines du culte Chrétien: Etude sur la liturgie latine avant Charlemagne.* Paris, E. Thorin, 1889.

Fisher, J.D.C. *Christian Initiation: Baptism in the Medieval West.* London, SPCK, 1965.

Gamber, K. "Der Taufritus nach dem Tassilo-Sakramentar." *Ecclesia Reginensis: Studien zur Geschichte und Liturgie der Regensburger Kirche im Mittelalter.* Studia Patristica et Liturgica, vol. 9. Regensburg, Friedrich Pustet, 1979, pp. 114-127.

Gros, M.S. "El antiguo ordo bautismal catalano-narbonense." *Hispania sacra* 28 (1975): 37-101.

Häring, N.M. "Commentaries on the Pseudo-Athanasian Creed." *Mediaeval Studies* 34 (1972): 208-252.

Jostes, M. "Der Dichter des Heliand." *Zeitschrift für Deutsches Altertum und Deutsche Litteratur* 40 (1896): 341-368.

Kolping, A. "Amalar von Metz und Florus von Lyons." *RB* 45 (1937): 108-118.

Kruse, N. *Die Kölner volksprachige Überlieferung des 9. Jahrhunderts.* Bonn, Rhemisches, 1976.

Lesvesque, J.L. "The Theology of the Post-Baptismal Rites in the VII and VIII Century Gallican Church." *EL* 95 (1983): 3-43.

Lynch, J.H. *Godparents and Kinship in Early Medieval Europe.* Princeton, NJ, Princeton University Press, 1986.

Mirgeler, A. *Kritischer Ruckblick auf das abenländische Christentum.* Freiburg im Breisgau, Herder, 1969.

Nocent, A. "Unzione e rinuncia nella tradizione liturgica romano-franco." *Ecclesia Orans* 2 (1985): 319-324.

--------. "Un fragment de sacramentaire de Sens au xe siècle: La liturgie baptismale de la province ecclésiastique de Sens dans les manuscrits du ixe au xvie siècles." *Miscellanea liturgica in onore de sua emineza il cardinale Giacomo Lercaro, arcivescovo di Bologna, presidente del 'Consilium' per l'applicazione della constituzione sulla sacra liturgia.* Vol. 2. Rome/Paris, Desclée, 1967.

Saxer, V. *Les rites de l'initiation chrétienne du IIe au VIe siècle: Esquisse historique et signification d'aprés leurs principaux témoins.* Centro Italiano di studi sull'alto medioevo, vol. 7. Spoleto, Centro Italiano di studi sull'alto medioevo, 1988.

Vogel, C. *La réform cultuelle sous Pepin le bref et sous Charlemagne.* Graz, Akademische, 1965.

3. On Charlemagne, the papacy and the metropolitans.

AA.VV., *Karl der Große (742-814).* Vienna, Wiener Katholische Akadamie, 1962.

Amann, E. *L'epoque carolinienne.* Fliche, A., Martin, V., eds. Histoire de l'Église depuis les origines jusqu'a nos jours, vol. 6. St. Dizier, Blond & Gay, 1937.

196

Barraclough, G. *The Medieval Papacy.* Library of European Civilization. London, Thames and Hudson, 1968 and 1979.

Beumann, H., Brunhölz, F., Winkelmann, W. *Karolus Magnus et Leo papa: ein Paderborner Epos vom Jahre 799.* Studien und Quellen zur Westfalischen Geschichte, vol. 8. Panderborn, Bonifacius, 1966.

Braunfels, W., gen. ed. *Karl der Grosse: Lebenswerk und Nachleben.* 5 vols. Düsseldorf, L. Schwann, 1965-1968.

Cabié, R. *The Sacraments.* Martimort, A.G., gen. ed., *The Church at Prayer*, vol. 3, new edn., O'Connell, M.J., trans. Collegeville, MN, The Liturgical Press, 1988.

Duchesne, L. *Fastes épiscopaux de l'ancienne Gaule.* Vol. 3: *Les provinces du Nord et de l'Est.* Paris, Fontemoing/E. DeBoccard, 1915.

Gadille, J., Fédou, R., Hours, H.,. De Vrégille, B. *Le diocèse de Lyon.* Plongeron, B., Vouchez, A., gen. eds. Histoire des diocèses de France, new series, vol. 16. Paris, Beauchesne, 1983.

Gams, P.B. *Series episcoporum Ecclesiæ catholicæ.* Regensburg, G.J. Manz, 1873.

Jedin, H., Dolan, J., Kempf, F., Beck, H.G., Ewig, E., Jungmann, J., gen. eds. *Handbook of Church History.* Vol 3: *The Church in the Age of Feudalism.* Biggs, A., trans. New York, Herder, 1969.

Jedin, H., Latourette, K.S., Martin, J. *Atlas zur Kirchengeschichte: Die christlichen Kirchen in Geschichte und Gegenwart.* Freiburg im Breisgau, Herder, 1970.

Lesne, E. *La hiérarchie épiscopale: provinces, métropolitains, primats en Gaule et Germanie depuis la réforme de saint Boniface jusqu'à la mort d'Hincmar, 742-882.* Mémoirs et travaux publiés par des professeurs des facultés catholiques de Lille, vol. 1. Lille/ Paris, A. Picard et fils, 1905.

Majo, A. *Storia della chiesa ambrosiana: Dalle origini ai nostri giorni.* Milian, Nuove Edizioni Duomo, 1995.

Navoni, M. "Dai Longobardi ai Carolingi." Caprioli, A., Rimolai, A., Vaccaro, L., eds., Storia Religiosa della Lombardia. *Diocesi di Milano*, vol. 1. Brescia, Editrice 'La Scuola', 1990.

Ohnsorge, W. "The Coronation and Byzantium." Sullivan, R.E., ed. and trans., *The Coronation of Charlemagne: What Did It Signify?* Problems in European Civilization, vol. 3. Boston, Heath, 1959.

Vetault, A. *Charlemagne.* 3rd edn. Tours, A. Mame et fils, 1888.

Wallace-Hadrill, J.M. *The Frankish Church.* Oxford History of the Christian Church,vol. 3. Oxford, Clarendon Press, 1983.

4. On Christian Initiation.

AA.VV., *Anàmnesis: Introduzione storico-teologica alla liturgia. Vol. 3/1: La liturgia, i sacramenti: Theologia e storia della celebrazione.* 2nd edn. Genova, Marietti, 1989.

AA.VV., *I simboli dell'Iniziazione christiana: Atti del I congresso internazional di liturgia, 25-28 maggio 1982.* Analecta Liturgica 7 = Studia Anselmiana 87. Rome, Pontificio Instituto Liturgico, 1984.

AA.VV., *Made, Not Born: New Perspectives on Christian Initiation and the Catechumenate.* The Murphy Center for Liturgical Research. Notre Dame, IN, University of Notre Dame Press, 1976.

Auf der Maur, H. and Kleinheyer B. eds. *Zeichen des Glaubens: Studien zu Taufe und Firmung: Balthasar Fischer zum 60. Geburstag.* Zurich/ Freiburg im Breisgau, Benziger/Herder, 1972.

Austin, G. *Anointing with the Spirit, the Rite of Confirmation: The Use of Oil and Chrism.* Studies in the Reformed Rites of the Catholic Church, vol. 3. New York, Pueblo, 1985.

Eliade, M. *Rites and Symbols of Initiation: The Mysteries of Birth and Rebirth.* Trask, W.R., Trans. New York, Harper and Row, 1965.

Fisher, J.D.C. *Confirmation, Then and Now.* London, SPCK, 1978.

Hammann, A. *Baptême et confirmation.* Paris, Desclée, 1969.

Kavanagh, A. *Confirmation: Origins and Reform.* New York, Pueblo, 1988.

--------. *The Shape of Baptism: The Rite of Christian Initiation.* Studies in the Reformed Rites of the Catholic Church, vol. 1. New York, Pueblo, 1978.

198

Kelly, H.A. *The Devil at Baptism: Ritual, Theology, Drama*. Ithaca, New York, Cornell Univeristy Press, 1985.

Lanne, E. "Les sacraments de l'initiation chrètienne et la confirmation dans l'église d'occident." *Irenikon* 57 (1984): 196-215, 324-326.

Lengeling, E.J. "Vom Sinn der Präbaptismalen Salbung." *Mélanges liturgiques offerts au R.P. dom Bernard Botte à l'occasion du cinquantième anniversaire de son ordination sacerdotale (4 Juin, 1972)*. Louvain, Abbaye du Mont César 1972: 327-358.

--------. "Der Exorzismus der katholishen Kirche." *Liturgisches Jahrbuch: Vierteljares hefte für Fragen des Gottesdienstes*, 32 (1982): 249-257.

Neunheuser, B. "De benedictione aquae baptismalis." *EL* 44 (1930): 194-207.

--------. *Taufe Und Firmung*. Schmaus, M., Geiselmann, J., Grillmeier, A., eds., Handbuch der Dogmengeschichte. Vol. 4: Sakramente, part 2. Freiburg im Breisgau, Herder, 1956.

Searle, M. *Christening: The Making of Christians*. Collegeville, MN, The Liturgical Press, 1980.

Steffen, U. *Taufe: Ursprung und Sinn des christlichen Einweihungsritus*. Stuttgart, Kreuz, 1988.

Stenzel, A. *Die Taufe: Eine genetische Erklärung der Taufliturgie*. Forschungen zur Geschichte der Theologie und des innerkirchlichen Lebens, vol. 7/8. Innsbruck, F. Rauch, 1958.

Vagaggini, C. *Theological Dimensions of the Liturgy: A General Treatise on the Theology of the Liturgy*. Doyle, L., Jurgens, W., trans. from the 4th Italian ed. Collegeville, MN, Liturgical Press, 1976.

Wainwright, G. *Christian Initiation*. Ecumenical Studies in History, vol. 10. London, Lutterworth, 1969.

--------. "The Rites and Ceremonies of Christian Initiation." *Studia Liturgica* 10 (1974): 2-24.

Whitaker, E.C., ed. *Documents of the Baptismal Liturgy*. 2nd ed. London, SPCK, 1970.

--------. *The Baptismal Liturgy.* Studies in Christian Worship, vol. 5. London, The Faith Press, 1965.

G. Winkler, "Confirmation or Chrismation?" *Worship* 58 (1984): 2-16.

5. General Reference Works.

Catholicisme: hier aujourd'hui demain. Paris, Letouyez et Ane, 1947- .

Dictionnaire d'archéologie chretienne et de liturgie. 15 vols. Paris, Letouyez et Ane, 1924-1953.

Dictionnaire d'histoire et géographie ecclésiastiques. Paris, Letouyez et Ane, 1912- .

Thesaurus Linguae Latinae editus iussu et auctoritate consilii ab academiis societatibusque diversarum nationum electi. Leipzig, B.G. Teubneri, 1900 - 1990.

Cattaneo, E. *Il culto cristiano in occidente: note storiche.* Bibliotheca "Ephemerides Liturgicae," "Subsidia," vol. 13. Rome, Centro liturgico Vincenziano, Edizioni liturgiche, 1978.

De Clercq, C., ed. *Dizionario det concili.* 6 vols. Vatican City, Città nuova, 1963-1967.

Denzinger, H., Schönmetzer, A., eds. *Enchiridion symbolorum, definitionum et declarationum de rebus fidei et morum.* 35th ed., emended. Freiburg in Breisgau, Herder, 1973.

Dix, G. *The Shape of the Liturgy.* 1st ed., London, A. & C. Black, 1945. Seabury ed., San Francisco, Harper and Row, 1982.

DuCange, C. *Glossarium mediae et infimae Latinitatis,* Carpenter, D.P., Henschel, G., supplement. New Edition. Favre, L., ed. Vol. 4. Graz, Austria, Akademischen, 1954.

Franz, A. *Die Kirchlichen Benedictionen in Mittelalter.* 2 vols., 2nd ed. Freiburg im Breisgau, Herder, 1909.

Jones, C., Wainwright, G., Yarnold, E., eds. *The Study of Liturgy.* New York, Oxford University Press, 1978.

King, A. *Liturgies of the Past*. Rites of the Western Church, vol. 4. London, Longman, Green and Company, 1959.

Neunheuser, B. *Storia della liturgia attraverso le epoche culturali*. Bibliotheca "Ephemerides Liturgicae," "Subsidia," vol. 11. Rome, Centro liturgico Vincenziano, Edizione Liturgiche, 1977.

Righetti, M. *Manuale di storia liturgica*. Vol. 4. Milan, Ancora, 1953.

Schäfer, T. *Die Fusswaschung im monastischen Brauchtum und in der Lateinischen Liturgie: Liturgiegeschichtliche Untersuchung*. Texte und Arbeiten, 1. Abteilung, vol. 47. Beuron, Beuroner Kunstverlag, 1956.

V. Thalhofer and L. Eisenhofer, *Handbuch der katholischen Liturgik*. Freiburg im Breisgau, Herder, 1933.

L. Weil, *Sacraments and Liturgy: The Outward Signs: A Study in Litugical Mentality*. Oxford, Blackwell, 1983.

Vogel, C. *Medieval Liturgy: An Introduction to the Sources*. Storey, W.G., Rasmsssen, N.K., revised and trans. Washington, D.C., The Pastoral Press, 1986.

Wegman, H. *Christian Worship in East and West: A Study Guide to Liturgical History*. Laythrop, G.W., trans. New York, Pueblo, 1985.

Index